Chip Kidd

MONOGRAPHICS

Véronique Vienne

Chip Kidd

Yale University Press

Published in North America by
Yale University Press
P.O. Box 209040
New Haven, CT 06520-9040

First published in Great Britain in 2003 by
Laurence King Publishing Ltd, London
Copyright © text 2003
Véronique Vienne

Library of Congress Control Number
2003104782

ISBN 0-300-09952-5

Designer: Brad Yendle, Design Typography,
London
Series editor: Rick Poynor
Additional photographer: Nigel Jackson
Printed in China

Frontispiece: from Chip Kidd, *Batman
Collected*. New York: Watson-Guptill
(paperback edition), 2001.

Contents

The Art of the Jester

Chip Kidd. Photograph by Duane Michals, 2001.

Pull a book at random from your bookcase and look at its cover. That is all you need to do to travel back to that specific moment in your life when you first read it. As compact as a time capsule, a book jacket holds forever the memory of the brief cultural period when it was in print. But a short shelf life is the price a book jacket must pay for leaving a vivid impression in the mind. My 1987 hardcover edition of Tom Wolfe's *The Bonfire of The Vanities*, so promising when it came out during the heady days of the Reagan administration, looks and feels today like a dear old friend wearing a toupee.[1] However, the fact that most book jackets look dated within a couple of years of their publication does not take anything away from their graphic appeal. One of the things we love about books is the way they age along with us.

Yet today, newness is considered a critical design element of a book jacket. Indeed, when I survey bookstores, the future obsolescence of the latest best-sellers' covers is the furthest thing from my mind. Even though I am aware that the current jackets will one day have the same emotional patina as award-winning jackets designed or art directed a decade ago by Louise Fili, Carin Goldberg, Sara Eisenman, Paula Scher, Frank Metz, Krystyna Skalski, Fred Marcellino or Neil Stuart, I cannot help but be seduced by the allure of instant modernity that the new books seem to capture. One of the things that tells me that a book is brand new is the presence of photography on its cover. Over the last couple of years, I have been conditioned to equate the use of conceptual photography on American book jackets with cutting-edge, contemporary literature. In contrast, if a book has an illustrated jacket, I regret to admit that I assume that its content is somewhat behind the curve. Graphic profiling, like racial profiling, is an inescapable reality in the world in which we live today.

The now popular photographic approach was originally pioneered in the late 1980s by a group of young designers working for the Knopf Publishing Group. Famous for its emblematic Borzoi logo, the Knopf imprint, a division of Random House, has always been a forward-thinking, design-conscious publishing venture. Founded in New York in 1915 by Alfred A. Knopf, a formidable *bon vivant* and bibliophile who loved music, history, sociology and nature preservation, the company had been, for the first 30 years of its existence, under the creative stewardship of lettering artist and woodcut illustrator William Addison Dwiggins.[2] Over the years, a prestigious roster of typographic mavericks including Paul Rand, Alvin Lustig, Warren Chappell, Bruce Rogers, Herbert Bayer and Lovat Frazer have designed books and jackets for the Knopf Publishing Group.

In 1986, Knopf went through a major transition. Bob Gottlieb, its long-time editor, left to run *The New Yorker* magazine, the celebrated yet financially bankrupted publication that Si Newhouse had acquired along with Random House. Replacing Gottlieb was Sonny Mehta, famous in the UK for his editorship of Picador. At the same time, coincidentally, the Knopf art department was going through a reorganization of its own. Sara Eisenman, then in charge, moved to Boston and Carol Devine Carson was brought in to replace her. In the shuffle, no one noticed the newly hired graphic designer who was doing his best to keep up with the demand for book covers. His name was Chip Kidd.

The man who is today a figurehead in the highbrow world of literary book jacket design was born Charles I. Kidd in 1964 in Shillington, Pennsylvania. His greatest design influence was daytime television. At age two, he was already a Batman fan, sporting as often as he could his superhero's costume, complete with mask, cape and gloves. A pure product of American pop culture, he developed a love of graphic design by staring in supermarkets at the packaging of Batman playthings – nightlights, belt buckles, action figures, pencil cases, water pistols and so on. At age 22, after graduating from Pennsylvania State University with a major in graphic design, he was hired at Knopf as a junior assistant to Sara Eisenman. In 2002, he had been on the Knopf payroll for 16 years, a tenure during which he has designed an average of 75 dust covers a year – altogether about 1,200 by his own accounting. His assignments come mainly from Knopf, but also from a wide range of clients, including HarpersCollins, Doubleday, Farrar, Straus & Giroux, Grove Press, Penguin/Putnam, Scribner and Columbia University Press. In America, it is not unusual for staff book jacket designers, who are notoriously underpaid, to freelance on the side. Taking full advantage of this loophole, Kidd has

run a thriving design practice from his desk at Knopf. But in exchange for his paycheck, he also serves as an editor-at-large at Pantheon, an imprint of Knopf, where he supervises the creation of graphic novels – illustrated narratives by comic strip artists – as well as one-of-a-kind projects, such as the recent coffee-table book on the art of Charles M. Schulz, the creator of *Peanuts*.

Chip Kidd has a reputation for designing covers that engage the readers' intelligence and imagination. Indeed, some of his best jackets are capable of triggering a moment of sheer insight into the nature of the text stowed between the covers. Others are simply elegant collages that suggest that this is the latest offering by a new talented writer. Because Kidd's name often appears on books that land on *The New York Times* best-sellers list, some authors even stipulate in their contract that he be the designer assigned to the cover of their book. Kidd has designed the jackets of scores of best-selling novels, including Michael Crichton's *Jurassic Park* (1990), Cormac McCarthy's *All the Pretty Horses* (1992), Michael Ondaatje's *The English Patient* (1992) and David Sedaris' *Naked* (1997).

52

60, 58

63

Today Kidd represents an odd phenomenon: an employee who gets more publicity than his employer. Content to be the maverick on the Knopf staff, he has avoided being promoted to a managerial position. But he has developed a persona that attracts media attention. A jack of all trades – designer, design critic, lecturer, editor – he has become a serious collector of Batman memorabilia and has edited a dozen books on, about or by cartoonists. His significant other is poet J.D. McClatchy, editor of *The Yale Review*, author of numerous books and a Chancellor of The Academy of American Poets. To top it all, Kidd's first novel, a coming-of-age story called *The Cheese Monkeys*, was published in 2001 and received critical acclaim, generating numerous interviews in both design publications and the mainstream press.[3]

106

Kidd's celebrity status is not all of his own making, even though his biographical brief – a one-paragraph blurb that is as carefully worded as a press release – states that his book jackets "have helped spawn a revolution in the art of American book packaging". Contrary to what some of his peers would like to believe, he does not have a personal publicist. His fame is the product of a culture that lionizes artists in order to turn them into commodities. Film, music, media and fashion personalities are not the only people who feed the gossip industry. During the 1990s, a handful of American designers have been singled out by the press and hailed as the next trendsetters. Fabien Baron, art director of *Harper's Bazaar*, was profiled in *The New York Times* and *The New Yorker*.[4] David Carson, of *Beach Culture* and *Ray Gun* fame, became a matinee idol in the graphic design field after the publication of his book, *The End of Print* (1995). Tibor Kalman, founder of M&Co, was interviewed by distinguished talk show host Charlie Rose in 1998. And an ever growing list of designers – the late Scott Makela, his wife Laurie, Stefan Sagmeister, John Maeda, Paula Scher, and now Chip Kidd – are revered by young designers as cultural icons, their personalities as compelling as their professional accomplishments.

Kidd has a winning public persona. A tall bespectacled figure, he looks like every college student's favourite roommate. "I think that the fact that my last name is 'Dick' spelled backwards really helps," he is likely to say to explain his popularity. He has perfected the stylized, sophomoric genre – he can keep you in stitches or, if you are not in the mood, get on your nerves by cracking one of his droll and well-rehearsed non sequiturs. "He has a great flair for the appropriate comment," remarked Milton Glaser. As a result, in the mainstream press, Kidd has been described as "a design demigod", "an inky colossus" and "the closest thing to a rock star".[5]

In this context, Kidd's high profile shouldn't raise eyebrows, but it does. His peers don't feel comfortable with his fame. On the one hand they envy his bravado and his willingness to be flamboyant in a field that used to be the domain of tweedy practitioners, but on the other hand they resent the fact that to compete with him, they can't be mere graphic designers any more, they also have to be perceived as multitalented, articulate, charming and funny. But there is a much more complicated reason why Kidd's visibility is a controversial topic among New York designers: he is only one of a group of talented people who are doing the kind of ground-breaking work he is given credit for. Among them are Michael Ian Kaye, who used to work for Farrar, Straus & Giroux, and who is now creative director at Little, Brown & Co. where he displays his well-tempered handling of typography; two former Knopf colleagues, Barbara de Wilde, with whom Kidd went to college, and Archie Ferguson, who is now head of the art department at Pantheon; John Gall and Robin Schiff, respectively at Vintage and Random House, where they art direct covers that win design awards year after year. Last but not least, Kidd's own boss, Carol Devine Carson, a formidable designer and the reason the Knopf imprint is still considered today a leader in the book jacket design field.

The now legendary Knopf jacket design team, photographed in 1992. From left to right: Archie Ferguson, Barbara de Wilde, Carol Carson and Chip Kidd. [6]

Always a gentleman, Kidd never misses an opportunity to praise the work of his peers, Carson included. Yet she declined to talk to me when I began to research Kidd's background. She was too busy, she said, and the list of questions I emailed to her in an attempt to cajole her were so open-ended, she couldn't bring herself to dignify them with an answer. I did not insist. Her boss, though, the legendary Sonny Mehta, editor-in-chief of Knopf, took it upon himself to clear things up. "I admire Chip immensely," he said, "but I want to be sure that you understand that Chip is not the only great designer at Knopf. They are all a terrific bunch, and they do exceptional work – all because of Carol's intelligence." Mehta is a savvy politician who knows how to get the best out of the people who work for him by challenging their ideas while accommodating their egos. He is particularly good at directing designers without stifling their creativity. He perfected his managerial style at Picador, which he launched in London in 1972 as an imprint of the Pan Group. There, between 1978 and 1986, he mentored a young designer, Gary Day-Ellison, giving him freedom to experiment by eschewing the cover approval committees that can drive into the ground the most inspired design concepts.[7] At the Knopf Publishing Group, where he supervises the Knopf imprint but also Pantheon Books, Vintage Books, Anchor Books, Schocken Books and Everyman's Library, Mehta plays the role of the visionary client, dictating the size and feel of a book, but letting his creative teams come up with unexpected design solutions for the jacket treatments.

Kidd is the first to admit that without Mehta's guidance he might not be the designer he is today. In particular, he appreciates the fact that he is given the freedom to choose which books he wants to work on. "The books Chip is drawn to are actually quite challenging, and edgy too," says Mehta. "He doesn't design jackets that are necessarily comforting, but they reflect his interest – and are always quite successful." In other words, Kidd's literary judgement is on par with his design talent. A book that appeals to him is likely to resonate with the sensibility of contemporary readers, and so will the cover he designs for it. Kidd's uncanny ability to pick winners is one of the reasons behind his successful career.

But the other reason is Carol Carson, an elegant designer with a distinctive style of her own. Kidd has learned a lot from her, and has integrated into his visual vocabulary one critical aspect of her work: her private passion for photography, which defines her approach to book design. "I like all kinds of photographs," Carson told me in 1999. "Fine art photography. Young people taking amazing pictures. Old vintage photographs. In fact I am addicted to photographs. I can't stop buying them!" Unwittingly, she stumbled on a novel idea: to illustrate fiction with photographs instead of illustrations. It was a sea-change in jacket design, one that everyone embraced, including Kidd. Unlike illustrated covers, which clearly broadcast the fact that a book is in the realm of fantasy, the photographic images give the impression that the story being told is about a non-fictional event. It is confusing, but intriguing. Today, the only detail that indicates that a text is written by a novelist, not a journalist, is the ten-point-type sign that says that the book is "a novel". This innovation, which Carson pioneered in the late 1980s after she was hired at Knopf, gave her work a look of sophistication. Thanks to photography, the stories told – fiction and non-fiction – all seemed more contemporary, endowed with an edgy realism that extolled the kind of narrative Sonny Mehta championed.

Before he learned to master the use of photography from Carson, Kidd gravitated toward typographical solutions. In 1989, he designed

the cover of Mehta's first acquisition, *Geek Love*, by Katherine Dunn.
A bright orange cover, it is strictly a typographical exercise, very
effective, but not a forerunner of the so-called "revolution in the art
of American book packaging" Kidd has since helped create. And even
though he has designed a number of jackets that only use type –
William Boyd's *Brazzaville Beach* (1991), Martin Amis' *London Fields* (1991),
Michael Crichton's *Disclosure* (1994) and Michael Lewis' *The New New
Thing* (1999), just to name a few – they are not among his most
arresting covers. His typographical approach is conceptual – he
chooses typefaces that evoke the mood, the style or the subculture
of the literary work he is promoting – but it is not graphically fine-
tuned. His handling of type betrays only a passing interest for font
design and typesetting subtleties. The relationship between the size,
the spacing and thickness of the characters on the page often falls flat.

    Today, even though Kidd sometimes relies on illustrations and
typography to bring out the personality of a writer, the jackets
that come to mind when mentioning his name usually involve
photographic images. Kidd figured out how to use the photographic
medium to define his own unique vision and for all her talent,
Carson is not as innovative as Kidd in her selection of photographs.
She gravitates toward images that complement the title of a book,
whereas Kidd stretches the visual boundaries between words and
visuals by choosing pictures that appear at first glance to be non
sequiturs. The jacket of David Shields' *A Handbook for Drowning* (1991)
shows an upside down figure standing against a huge cloudy sky;
the hardcover jacket of James Ellroy's *White Jazz* (1992) features the
bullet-ridden door of a police car; the image on McCarthy's cover for
The Crossing (1994) is a sepia photograph of horses' skulls.

    By distancing the title from the image on the cover, Kidd puts a
very specific kind of pressure on readers: he asks them to bridge
the gap between what they read and what they see. In the process
he empowers them by demanding they take control of the
communication. This approach is reminiscent of the Sense-Making
methodology developed by cognition theorist Brenda Dervin who,
for the last two decades, has studied how people seek information
and muddle through contradictions and discontinuities to reach
conclusions.[8] By acknowledging that most of us construct meaning
by bridging gaps in our understanding, she adds credence to the
postmodern notion that the reader is the rightful author of the
"text", as defined by Roland Barthes. This could explain why

26
34
53
71
48
61

photographic covers appeal to contemporary readers more than illustrated ones. While illustrations are intentionally constructed to illuminate specific points of a "text", fine art photographs – the kind that are favoured by jacket designers – contain serendipitous elements that leave the image open to interpretation. This deliberate lack of definition testifies to the postmodern expectations of a public increasingly more familiar with avant-garde mannerisms.

A couple of other cultural trends helped propel photography on the covers of works of fiction. One was the growing popularity of black and white photographs in the status-conscious 1980s, when fashion magazines, eager to recapture the glamour of the past, were reproducing vintage prints by the likes of Cecil Beaton, Erwin Blumenfeld, Toni Frissell, Horst P. Horst, George Hoyningen-Huene, Adolph de Meyer and Edward Steichen. Inspired by the timeless minimalism of these stylized pictures, young photographers began to shoot in black and white, experimenting with large format cameras, short lenses and long exposures. The images they created were a welcome relief from the heavy-handed colour photography that was considered "high-tech" at the time. Tempered by a modern sensibility, the nostalgic simplicity of these newly minted black and white images appealed to a wide audience enamoured with the allure of retro styles.

The other trend was the proliferation of stock photography, due in part to the growing demand for the kind of fine art, black and white photographs published in trendy fashion magazines. Whereas traditional stock photography offered the most stereotypical images, in the 1990s, stock houses began to put together collections of photographs usually found in downtown galleries. This was a godsend for book cover designers who now had access to ready-made evocative images that could be used to create overnight mock-ups for cover concepts. More seductive than sketches, the roughed-out photographic covers were approved by editors and by authors who liked the "finished" look of the ideas presented to them. Little by little, photographic covers for works of fiction gained acceptance in publishing circles.

Chip Kidd seldom resorts to stock photography, but he is a proponent of found images. He haunts flea markets, looking for old prints and yellowed family snapshots. He finds strange portraits in the back of junk stores and intriguing prints in secondhand bookstores. He is likely to hold on to an image for years, until the day when the right manuscript comes along and the odd picture suddenly takes on a new meaning of its own. One example of this is the cover for *The Abomination* by Paul Golding (2000), a novel about the emotional alienation of a gay childhood. Kidd was in the middle of reading the manuscript – something he does slowly over a period of a month – when he got a postcard in the mail with a black and white picture of a stuffed toy bunny standing on its head, by photographer Lars Klove. "It's nothing I ever would have thought of using," he remembers, "but it made perfect sense to me." His design was straightforward, but powerful. The words "the abomination", simply reversed against the plain background of the image, functioned as a caption – with just enough of a sinister overtone to turn an innocent picture into an ill-boding icon. At first, Paul Golding's agent refused to show the bunny cover to his client. Kidd tried a series of new approaches, but no one liked them. After eight months, the agent backed down and showed the original cover to Golding who was so taken by it that he wrote Chip Kidd a two-page letter explaining why he loved it. Today, both Carol Carson and Sonny Mehta think that *The Abomination* is one of Kidd's best covers.[9]

Typical of Alvin Lustig's modernist collage approach, this jacket for a book of plays by Garcia Lorca was designed in the late 1940s for New Directions Inc., a New York publisher.

"Looking at book jackets is like watching TV without the sound," Kidd explains. "It's like being in a bar, or at the gym, and watching the news on the TV monitor without being able to hear anything. In that situation, even the most benign photograph of a smiling kid can spell disaster. You instantly imagine the worst-case scenario." Like communication theorist Brenda Dervin, Kidd believes that we decode random imagery all the time, picking bits and pieces of information here and there to construct coherent images in our mind. That is why he uses what he calls "the magpie method".[10] He picks, chooses and borrows images and visual tricks and makes something new out of them. His approach is not unlike that of book designer Alvin Lustig, to whom he is sometimes compared. Like Lustig in the 1940s, Kidd fragments the narrative on the jacket, his compositions breaking up the picture into pieces of a visual and verbal puzzle. His cover for Geoff Ryman's *Was* (1992), a revisionist fantasy of *The Wizard of Oz*, is a pleasing patchwork of five photographs reminiscent of a famous five-image cover by Alvin Lustig for a book of tragedies by Lorca.

At the beginning of his career, Kidd favoured two-image collages, so much so that he was known to insiders as "the guy who splits his covers into two equal rectangles". It was an almost fail-proof formula. Sometimes one of the rectangles carried the title, the other the image, for example, *White Jazz* by James Ellroy (1992); *My Hard Bargain* by

64
60
61, 61
70
83
28

Walter Kirn (1990); *The New Testament*, translated by Richmond
Lattimore (1996); and Cormac McCarthy's trilogy, *All the Pretty Horses*
(1992), *The Crossing* (1994) and *Cities of the Plain* (1998). Sometimes two
photographs shared the field, each in its own box (*Turn of the Century*
by Kurt Andersen, 1999). And sometimes the jacket was split into
vertical panels (*Mixing Messages* by Ellen Lupton for the Cooper-Hewitt
National Design Museum, 1996 and *The Day Room* by Don DeLillo, 1987).

This panel-to-panel approach to the narrative brings to mind
the comic book format, particularly since Kidd has had a lifelong
fascination with the Batman mythology. In *Understanding Comics* (1993),
Scott McCloud explains that the panel itself is the comic's most
important icon.[11] "The space between the panels … plays host to
much of the magic and mystery that are at the very heart of the
comics," he writes. "Here, in the limbo [between the panels] human
imagination takes two separate images and transforms them into a
single idea."[12] Panel-to-panel narratives are powerful because they
compel readers to fill in the blanks between the seen and the unseen,
the visible and the invisible – or as Dervin would say, between
"discontinuities". The result is viewer participation – exactly what a
Chip Kidd cover tries to elicit. Instead of just defining a surface, his
jackets define a time sequence during which the mind races between
the various panels, putting together bits and pieces of visual and
verbal information. His covers are successful when, upon completing
this act of creation, the viewer comes away with a greater awareness
of what he or she thinks the book is about.

This is the case for Kidd's favourite cover, *The New Testament*, which
he designed in 1996 for Farrar, Straus & Giroux. The upper panel
displays the title and the name of a translator, while the lower panel
is an extreme close-up of a dead man's face, his fixed gaze staring
into space. Taken by Andres Serrano, the artist notorious for his
photograph of a crucifix in a glass of urine, the image of this Christ
figure is hauntingly beautiful. "Pieces of faces always work well on
book jackets," says Kidd. "Partial images have the same emotional
impact as the entire image, but they are less literal." Partial images
also lend mystery to Kidd's layouts: the missing or obstructed piece
of a photograph suggests that there is a lot more to the narrative
than meets the eye. For this reason, he often runs type over the most
interesting detail of a picture, or crops a face in half, or shows the
back rather than the front of an object or a figure, or enlarges a
texture beyond recognition. Sometimes he does all of the above at

17

On this page from *Understanding Comics*
by Scott McCloud, the author/cartoon
character explains that "the panel acts
as a sort of general indicator that time
or space is being divided."

once, and as a result his covers become complex tapestries that are
both provocative and pleasing to the eye (*Darling* by William Tester,
1991), yet are somehow less evocative than his simpler collages.
Whenever he attempts to outdo himself, Kidd defeats his purpose,
which is, ultimately, to sell books.

30

If the photographs used by Kidd on jackets are not partially
cropped or covered, they are sometimes blurry – another trick of the
trade many designers resort to as an alternative to give photographs
a less literal signature. In collaboration with photographer Geoff
Spear, a master of the macro lens, Kidd has perfected a shallow depth
of field approach that allows him to focus on the sensual details of an
object while letting the rest of the image drop off into a blurry haze.
One of the first covers he did with Spear was for *The Pencil* by Henry
Petroski, published by Knopf in 1990. Only the lead point of the yellow
pencil is in sharp focus, while the rest of the image is steeped in a
warm and fuzzy glow. Since, Spear has shot more than 20 covers for
Kidd, including *The Night Manager* (1993) by John LeCarré, designed by
Kidd and Carson, and showing an old-fashioned book jacket in
the chiaroscuro of a lamplight, its letterpress typography so

68

realistically photographed you want to touch it; *The Wind-Up Bird
Chronicle* (1997) by Haruki Murakami, displaying an extreme close-up
of a tin bird, its painted eye smack in the middle of the front cover,
while the rest of its body wraps around the book in a blurry swirl of
abstract curves; and, more recently, *Let Nothing You Dismay* (1998) by
Mark O'Donnell, featuring a Christmas plastic lawn ornament bathed
in the radiant haze of its internal light.

This type of imagery, which emphasizes the three-dimensional
quality of an object, appeals to Kidd who likes to "make things". As
much as possible, he tries to turn the flat surface of a jacket into an
artifact. No sleight of hand is too contrived for him: translucent

44

overlays, die-cuts, trompe l'oeils – you name it. The cover of *Nothing
If Not Critical* (1992) by art critic Robert Hughes is a trompe l'oeil of the
back of a canvas, complete with staples and hanging wires. *The Shock
of The New* (1991), by the same author, has an embossed fluorescent
label stuck over the title that advertises the newness of "The New".

53

The jacket of Michael's Crichton's *Disclosure* (1994) is a thick vellum
that partially obscures the title printed on the case below. The jacket

63

of David Sedaris' *Naked* (1997), on which you see a realistic photograph
of a pair of men's shorts, is cropped on top to reveal the title. Slip it
off – as you would when undressing – and you see underneath it the

41 X-ray of a pelvis. On the jacket of *The Book of the Penis* (2000) by Maggie Paley, the fig leaf (which looks more like an English ivy leaf) can be lifted off – something Kidd says he has never been able to resist doing.

The intricate cleverness of these jackets gives the impression that Kidd is frustrated with the limitations of his medium. He uses every surface of a hardcover jacket – the spine, the back, the flaps – to escape from the two-dimensional world of graphic design. Sometimes, if he is lucky, he gets a crack at designing the inside of a book, as he 36 did with *Watching the Body Burn* (1989) by Thomas Glynn, which he curiously adorned with his own cartoon-like drawings. The jacket and the book seem to merge, with the first chapter beginning on the cover and continuing on the front flap, while the illustrations of the jacket reappear playfully on chapter openings. But no book is as elaborate as 106 the one Chip designed for his own literary debut, *The Cheese Monkeys: A Novel in Two Semesters*, published in 2001 by Scribner.[13] There, he attempts to change all the rules, including the ones of his own making. He uses photographs, but they are photographs of a collage made of bits and pieces of illustrations that are so realistically captured by Geoff Spear's macro lens that the result looks like a pastiche. The jacket is a sleeve that slides to reveal the case on which the title has been reinterpreted as a rebus by illustrator Chris Ware. The spine proclaims "Good Is Dead", almost obliterating the title of the book. The sides of the pages have been stained with a double cryptic message, depending which way you look at it – "Good Is Dead", if you flip the pages from the front, and "Do You See?" if you flip them from the back. The acknowledgements run along the edge of the book, precariously straddling the binding. And that is just the beginning. Suffice it to say that inside, the text is set in two different typefaces (Apollo and Bodoni), one for each of the two "semesters".

Only a private investigator would be able to decipher the meaning of all the visual clues with which Kidd likes to bait the reader. One thing is sure: his obsessive imagination has been shaped by comic book detective stories – by the characters of the DC (Detective Comics) series in particular. "I am a sucker for the false promises of comic books," he once said in an interview.[14] Like the Caped Crusader, his favourite superhero, Kidd likes to wear a mask. You are never quite sure of what he means – and whether he sincerely means it. "I never really know if the readers get the subtle visual puns of my jackets," he says. "But I can't let that inform my design to the point where I will compromise." His work with comic books is an example of how

When he saw this image in photographer Geoff Spear's portfolio, Kidd vividly recalled seeing it previously in a book of songs by Talking Heads. Since then, the Kidd/Spear collaboration has been most prolific.

ABOVE AND OPPOSITE As a boy, Kidd was fascinated by the packaging of Batman playthings and action figures, which he began to collect when he was three. He now believes that he learned some of his most valuable lessons in graphic design in toy stores. 15

far he is willing to go to avoid compromising his vision. Often acting as archivist, editor, art director and writer – sometimes not even paid for it – Kidd has created a number of illustrated books on various cartoon characters – Batman of course, but also Superman, Wonder Woman, Plastic Man and the Peanuts gang. His collaboration with Geoff Spear reached new heights when he endeavoured to photograph hundreds of toys, action figures, play sets, costumes, trading cards, board games, model kits, colouring books, posters, decoders, pins, lunch boxes, nightlights, snow globes, ashtrays and jelly jars from his own collection, as well as from the collections of comic book fans nationwide.

Using a chiaroscuro lighting technique that brings out not only the texture of the paper, but also every minute scratch, blemish and tear that give old comic books and artifacts their nostalgic character, Chip and Geoff have so far compiled the visual material for six such books. Only *Jack Cole and Plastic Man* (2001), written by Art Spiegelman, the creator of *Maus*, and published by Chronicle, was not photographed by Spear for budgetary reasons.

You do not have to be a comic book fan to appreciate the artistry of these colourful tomes. Even I, who years ago, out of boredom, walked out of one of Chip Kidd's lectures on Batman, take immense pleasure studying every single spread of these compendiums. They are a

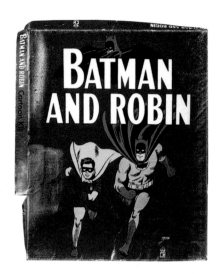

showcase for Kidd's ability to bring out the emotional content of images through bold, panel-to-panel juxtapositions. In this context, Geoff Spear's dramatic photographs, often shot against brightly coloured backgrounds, acquire a cinematic dimension. Their latest book, *Peanuts: The Art of Charles M. Schulz* (2001), is probably their finest collaboration so far. At the invitation of the executors of the Charles Schulz's estate, Kidd and Spear spent two weeks in California photographing the late cartoonist's archives. Combining these pictures with photographs of early vintage strips from illustrator Chris Ware's collection, they created a fluid visual narrative that pays homage to the man who gave us *Good Grief! Charlie Brown*.

For Kidd, Pantheon is a second home within the Knopf Publishing Group. With editorial director Dan Frank, he has helped develop there the successful "graphic novels division", an informal publishing venture that puts out unusual books by up-and-coming cartoonists. It all started in the early 1980s with the serendipitous publication of Matt Groening's *Life in Hell*. Then, in 1986, Louise Fili, who was then the art director of Pantheon, convinced an editor to publish the now internationally acclaimed *Maus* by Art Spiegelman. Since then, every new graphic novel published by Pantheon has had a loyal following in spite of the initial resistance of booksellers who did not know where to place these hybrid books in their stores. According to Dan Frank,

The intricate jacket of Chris Ware's *Jimmy Corrigan*, which Kidd lovingly shepherded from beginning to end, but did not design, is a folded poster wrapped around an old-fashioned case. "Everyone who sees this book cover says it's *amazingly* beautiful," notes Kidd. "I wish I'd done it, but it's all Chris' work."

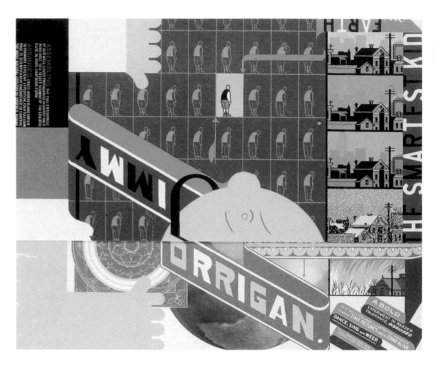

Peter Saville's design for New Order's *Low-life* album (Factory Records, 1985) is among Kidd's favourite design artifacts. Part of the image is printed on a vellum slipcover, a technique Kidd uses with great success in some of his own jacket designs, notably *The Secret History* by Donna Tartt and *Disclosure* by Michael Crichton.

the main credit for the success of the Pantheon graphic novels should go to Kidd because the artists he works with – Chris Ware, Daniel Clowes, Ben Katchor – trust him as an editor. In close collaboration with the production department, Kidd makes sure that each illustrated book is as distinctive as its author wants it to be. The most unusual book to date is probably Chris Ware's *Jimmy Corrigan* (2002), a comic strip whose hero is a doughy, middle-aged loser who thinks he is "The Smartest Kid on Earth".[16] An intricate tapestry of minutely detailed drawings, the book, designed by Chris Ware, is wrapped in a jacket that is a folded poster covered with stamp-like illustrations and four-point-type disclaimers. Upon the insistence of the notoriously shy Chris Ware, his name is nowhere to be found, expect on the spine, where it is almost illegible, printed upside down. "It was no fun to go into Sonny's office with that jacket and have him say 'where's the author's name and why is half the title upside down?'" Chip Kidd remembers. But that is just the kind of battle he likes to fight in order to promote the work of the cartoonists he so admires.

"Comics are my Mr. Hyde to the Knopf Dr. Jekyll," Kidd says to explain his dual career. But people who know him well see no

This poster is by Lanny Sommese, Kidd's most influential teacher at Penn State University. Sommese's work is "more reminiscent of European printmaking and graphic illustration than of American sources," writes Philip B. Meggs. "[He] photographed hundreds of wood engravings from nineteenth-century science magazines, which he later used in surreal collages." [17]

contradiction in his two-sided talent. Barbara de Wilde, who studied graphic design at Penn State with Kidd and worked in close collaboration with him at Knopf for almost 15 years, thinks that the two aspects of his work are actually closely related. "Comic books are very complicated, and they are miraculous," she says, adding that the verve, the irony and the cleverness that is in Kidd's jackets is also in comic books. She believes that it is people like Kidd – the slightly nerdy types who go to comic books conventions – who turn out to be smarter than all of us because they can read between the lines. They are the outsiders who get the inside jokes.

The inside joke is what graphic artist Lanny Sommese, who was Kidd's and de Wilde's favourite teacher at Penn State, would call a "visual-verbal" connection. "The verbal opens up the meaning of the visual, and the visual opens up the meaning of the verbal," he explains. In Kidd's work, he adds, both meanings are open-ended, forcing the viewer to fill in the blanks. Coming up with "visual-verbal" design solutions was central to Sommese' teaching method. Reminiscent of the Sense-Making approach of Dervin, it was in fact based on ideas expressed by Arthur Koestler, in *The Act of Creation*. [18] In it, the Hungarian-born British novelist compares creativity with what he calls jest. Jest is the mental leap one must make in order to get a joke. Requiring instant audience participation, jest is one of the most effective forms of communication.

At Penn State, Kidd was indeed a jester – a quipster, a prankster. Not surprisingly, his favourite Batman villain is the Joker, an "almost loveable egomaniac" who is torn between two ambitions, comedy and crime. [19] And indeed, Barbara de Wilde remembers Kidd as a clown, as "someone who was never afraid to make a fool of himself", yet who was a wide-eyed and caring individual. Already back then, she had noticed that her friend showed a taste for compartmentalizing his life into antithetical opposites. He could be both edgy and good-natured, blasé and naïve, irreverent and candid. In the graphic design department, where he hung around people who worked hard at being cool, his hero was bad-boy British record-cover designer Peter Saville, a seminal figure in the music industry avant-garde in the 1980s. Yet, at the same time, Kidd was able to embrace the local, small-town culture of Penn State without reservation. A dedicated member of the rah-rah college marching band, he was a consummate drummer, pounding on his three-piece drum set with both enthusiasm and finesse.

23

Kidd recently revealed yet another of his talents by demonstrating that he was a writer as well as a designer. A thinly veiled autobiographical account of his college days, *The Cheese Monkeys* lies somewhere between adolescent derision and design manifesto – *Catcher in The Rye* meets *First Things First*. He laboured on his novel for years, working at nights and over weekends. His partner, J.D. McClatchy, was on hand to provide support, even though fiction writing is not a genre he is particularly fond of. But Kidd and McClatchy shared a common experience, one which is central to the plot of *The Cheese Monkeys*: they both have been under the spell of a great teacher in college – Harold Bloom teaching poetry at Yale for McClatchy and Lanny Sommese teaching graphic design at Penn State for Kidd – and they both had to overcome their devotion to their mentors in order to find their own voice. It was not easy. Both teachers were charismatic and abusive. Bloom's classroom manners were "deliberately provocative, at once gripping and infuriating", according to McClatchy.[20] In Kidd's novel, the fictional Sommese, named Winter Sorbeck, is a larger-than-life character who looks like Gary Cooper's fraternal twin: "He was big. Not fat, not at all. Big. Like a cliff you were just pushed from."[21]

One cannot help but wonder if, for Kidd, reinventing himself as a writer is not like jumping off a cliff. The relentless bantering style of his novel gives the impression that the author is someone on the verge of breakdown, or maybe on the verge of a breakthrough. Indeed, as successful as he is, Kidd probably feels that he needs to make a leap forward to stay ahead of his game. By authoring a novel, he is hurling himself into the unknown – literally pushing the envelope and breaking out of the wrapping. Already, he has a couple of sequels in mind for his novel, and maybe he would like to write film scripts. And if he gets his way, years from now, he will probably be too involved with his own writing to design the jackets of his books.

Selected Work

GEEK LOVE

A NOVEL

KATHERINE DUNN

"A Fellini movie in ink. . . . *Geek Love* throws a punch."
—SAN FRANCISCO CHRONICLE

Geek Love
Katherine Dunn
1989 New York ALFRED A. KNOPF
[Hardback]

The story of parents deliberately breeding
human mutants for exhibition in a
sideshow is so perverse it could hardly
be conveyed by conventional means.
The purely graphic solution – an explosive
mix of typography and colour – is as
disquieting as this bizarre tale of freakish
family values.

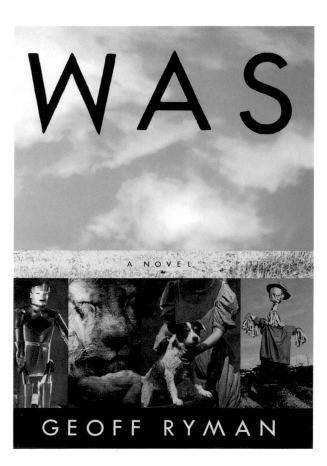

Was
Geoff Ryman
Photographs – Bettman Archives
and Geoff Spear
1992 New York ALFRED A. KNOPF
[Hardback]

"Although the story of the Wizard of Oz
by L. Frank Baum is in the public domain,"
explains Kidd, "MGM's movie version
of the same definitely is not. How then to
depict its characters (prominently featured
in *Was*) without harkening to Judy & Co.?"[1]

Who's Irish
Gish Jen
Photograph – Stephanie Rausser
1999 New York ALFRED A. KNOPF
[Hardback]

In these stories Jen examines the
immigrant experience and the different
ethnic groups that share that journey.
The cover photograph alludes to the fact
that children, in all cultures, are always
more adaptable than adults because they
are willing to look at the world upside
down. "It's hard to believe they approved
this one," remarks Kidd, "but I think that
it truly captures the spirit of the story,
which is sort of impish free for all."[2]

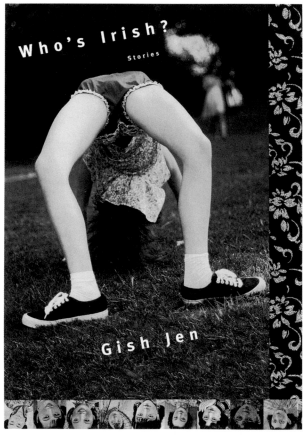

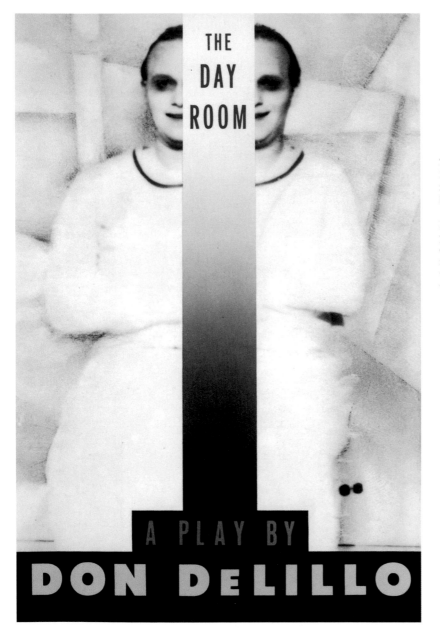

THE
DAY
ROOM

A PLAY BY

DON DeLILLO

The Day Room
Don DeLillo
1987 New York ALFRED A. KNOPF
[Hardback]

In this complicated and challenging play, the author explores the meaning of reality and illusion. The baffling cover image, split abruptly in two, prepares the reader for DeLillo's relentless and uncomfortable probing.

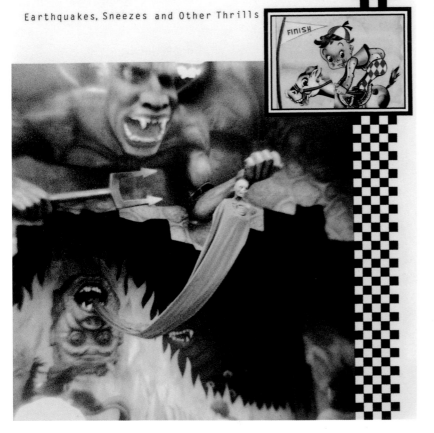

WILD RIDE

BIA LOWE

Earthquakes, Sneezes and Other Thrills

Wild Ride   29
Bia Lowe
Photograph – Deborah Sugarman
1995 New York HARPERCOLLINS
[Hardback]

These stories are a mad jumble of thrilling
experiences; sometimes ordinary,
sometimes extraordinary, but always vivid.
Kidd's hyperactive cover mixes unsettling
touches of the grotesque and the precious.

Darling

William Forster

Knopf

ISBN 0-394-56872-9

9 780394 568720

51800>

Darling
William Tester
Photograph – Geoff Spear
1991 New York ALFRED A. KNOPF
[Hardback]

Two young brothers become rivals for the
love of a cow in this bizarre and original
tale. The cover receives an equally bizarre
and original juxtaposition of pattern,
image and jerky, child-like calligraphy.
The relentless scrawling of "Darling"
over and over is an indication of the dark
obsession that runs right through this tale.

The Secret History
Donna Tartt
Designed with Barbara de Wilde
1992 New York ALFRED A. KNOPF
[Hardback]

"We were most impressed by the novel's ability to combine classical and modern sensibilities," explains Kidd, "and wanted the design to set it apart from its competition. We took a cue from antiquarian booksellers, who often wrap their more precious volumes in a jacket of clear acetate. Ours, though, would be imprinted with typographic information in a modern face and lie on top of an antiquated image."[3]

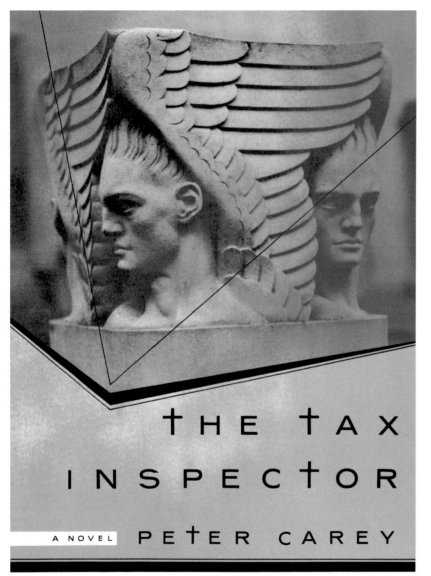

The Tax Inspector
Peter Carey
1993 New York ALFRED A. KNOPF
[Hardback]

This family saga hinges on a character's
demented identification with angels
and on the arrival of a tax inspector.
Kidd searched for an image that would
combine the solidity of bureaucracy
with the otherwordliness of the angelic.
This carving, which he describes as
"Federalist in mood" looks as if it was
taken from the hallowed halls of some
government building.

34

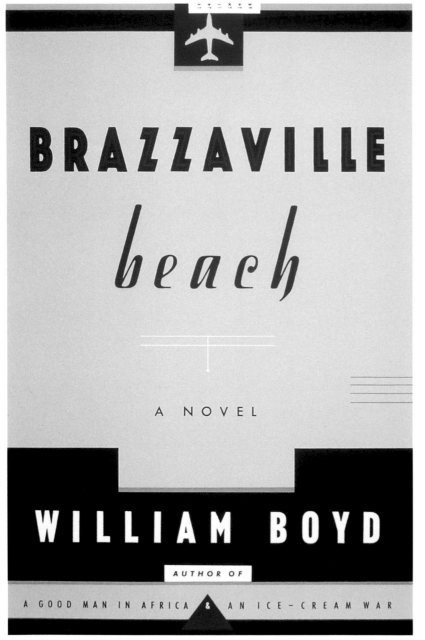

BRAZZAVILLE
beach

A NOVEL

WILLIAM BOYD

AUTHOR OF

A GOOD MAN IN AFRICA & AN ICE-CREAM WAR

Brazzaville Beach
William Boyd
1991 New York WILLIAM MORROW & CO.
[Hardback]

Since the protagonist in the novel smokes
an exotic brand of cigarettes, Kidd decided
to imagine what the pack might look like.
"Seen from a distance, most books have
the appearance of cigarette packs anyway,"
he says.[4]

WILLIAM BOYD

THE

Blue

AFTERNOON

a novel

The Blue Afternoon
William Boyd
Designed with Carol Devine Carson
1995 New York ALFRED A. KNOPF
[Hardback]

This sweeping tale set in the Philippines at the turn of the century is told in flashback by a father to his long-lost daughter. Kidd manages to conjure up the exotic mood of the novel thanks to the celadon green background reminiscent of Asian glazed pottery. The iconic fan alludes both to the complex social niceties of the time and the romantic intrigues of the plot.

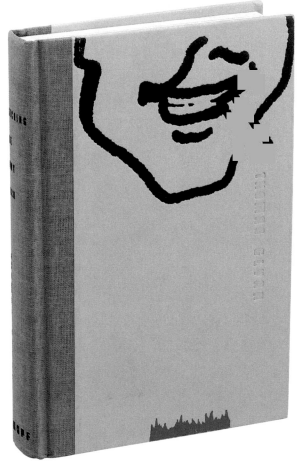

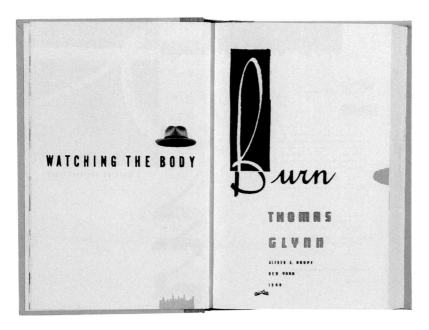

Watching the Body Burn
Thomas Glynn
Illustrations – Chip Kidd
1989 New York ALFRED A. KNOPF
[Hardback]

Designed and illustrated by Chip Kidd,
the cover attempts to capture the narrative
style of Thomas Glynn's audacious novel in
which a son tells of the decline and decay
of his father's life in startling and often
shocking language. Uncharacteristically,
Kidd also designed the inside of the book,
carrying the visual theme all the way
through. Note the burning Knopf Borzoi
logo on the title page and on the spine of
the dust jacket.

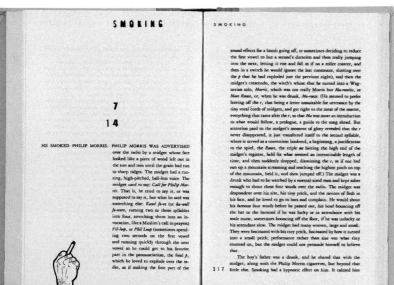

The Actual Adventures of Michael Missing
Michael Hickins
Illustrations – Charles Burns
1991 New York ALFRED A. KNOPF
[Hardback]

This debut collection of eleven short
stories tells of eleven troubled young men,
all named Michael Missing. Kidd plays up
the daring quality of the protagonists with
a noirish illustration, while the bloody
colours of the background heighten the
dramatic tension.

38

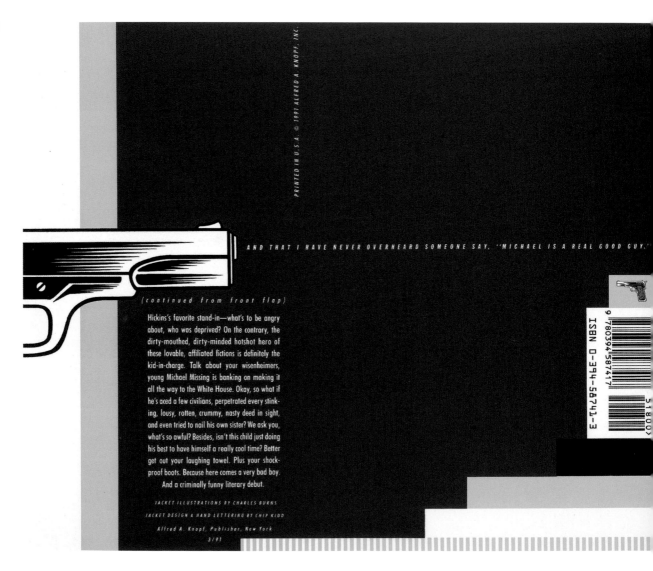

PRINTED IN U.S.A. © 1991 ALFRED A. KNOPF, INC.

AND THAT I HAVE NEVER OVERHEARD SOMEONE SAY, "MICHAEL IS A REAL GOOD GUY."

(continued from front flap)

Hickins's favorite stand-in—what's to be angry
about, who was deprived? On the contrary, the
dirty-mouthed, dirty-minded hotshot hero of
these lovable, affiliated fictions is definitely the
kid-in-charge. Talk about your wisenheimers,
young Michael Missing is banking on making it
all the way to the White House. Okay, so what if
he's aced a few civilians, perpetrated every stink-
ing, lousy, rotten, crummy, nasty deed in sight,
and even tried to nail his own sister? We ask you,
what's so awful? Besides, isn't this child just doing
his best to have himself a really cool time? Better
get out your laughing towel. Plus your shock-
proof boots. Because here comes a very bad boy.
      And a criminally funny literary debut.

JACKET ILLUSTRATIONS BY CHARLES BURNS
JACKET DESIGN & HAND LETTERING BY CHIP KIDD
Alfred A. Knopf, Publisher, New York
3/91

ISBN 0-394-58741-3
9 780394 587417
51800>

FPT U.S.A. $18.00   Canada $23.50

Michael Hickins lives in Paris now. But he was born in a particularly unlovely precinct of Queens, one of the five boroughs constituting the City of New York—and it was there in the hardpan of Queens that Hickins went to school in the lessons of the street and in the higher learning of the back room. A scholarship sent him to Columbia, where he acquired an interest in making a record of what he knew. The result is this book. But do not look in it for the kind of report one has come to expect from the formerly angry, the hitherto deprived. Because to see it the way Michael Missing sees it—Michael Missing being Michael

(c o n t i n u e d   o n   b a c k   f l a p)

MICHAEL
HICKINS

THE
Actual
ADVENTURES *of* MICHAEL MISSING

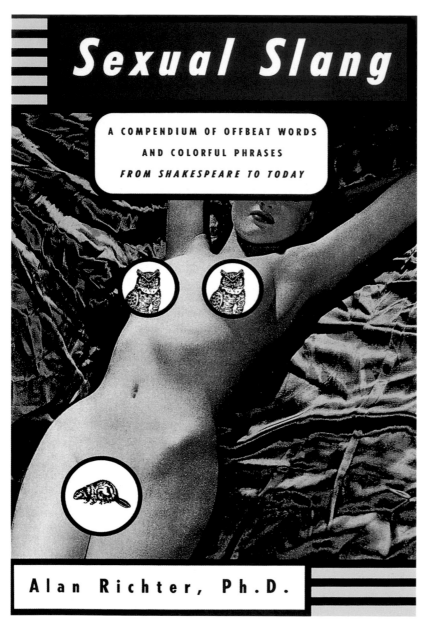

Sexual Slang
Alan Richter
1995 New York HARPERCOLLINS
[Paperback]

For this compendium of sexual expressions, Kidd chose wholesome pin-ups strategically covered with punning line drawings, setting a tone that eliminates any possibility of embarrassment for potential bookstore browsers. This cover was available in male and female versions, of course.

The Book of the Penis
Maggie Paley
Photograph – Chip Kidd
2000 New York GROVE PRESS
[Hardback]

Mocking our prurient curiosity, the leaf
on this cover actually lifts up but reveals
nothing. Readers must go to the text itself
for just about every medical, cultural and
historical fact known about the male
member in different cultures, historical
periods and circumstances. Men's pre-
occupation with penile size is knowingly
mocked by the ruler along the spine.

Peppers
Amal Naj
Illustration – Chip Kidd
1992 New York ALFRED A. KNOPF
[Hardback]

This jacket reflects the defining qualities
of the book's subject matter – hot peppers.
Bold, graphic and colourful it acts as a
wake-up call to the senses.

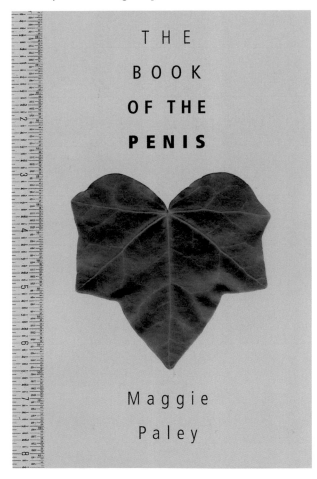

42 *The American Replacement of Nature*
William Irwin Thompson
Designed with Barbara de Wilde
1991 New York DOUBLEDAY
[Hardback]

The scale of the face and the cropping
of the image create a billboard effect
that is in keeping with the tone of the
book, a frightening examination of
how technology and the media are de-
humanizing our perceptions of reality,
nature, education and culture.

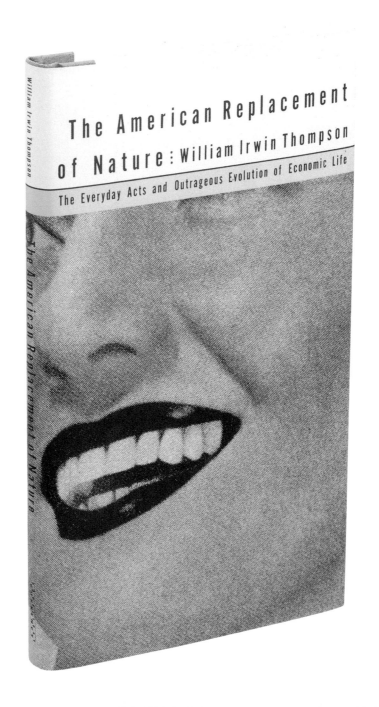

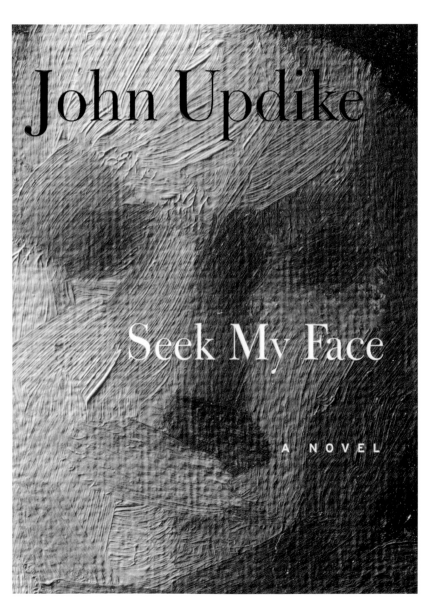

Seek My Face   43
John Updike
Photograph – Geoff Spear
2002 New York ALFRED A. KNOPF
[Hardback]

A fictional day-long interview with a
painter, the novel captures the mood
of postwar American art in the heyday
of Abstract Expressionism. Kidd asked
Spear to photograph a detail of a small
painting he had found at an art students'
gallery exhibition. Eye-catching from
a distance, the face on the jacket
becomes a blur of brushstrokes as you
get closer, giving the title *Seek My Face*
a graphic resonance.

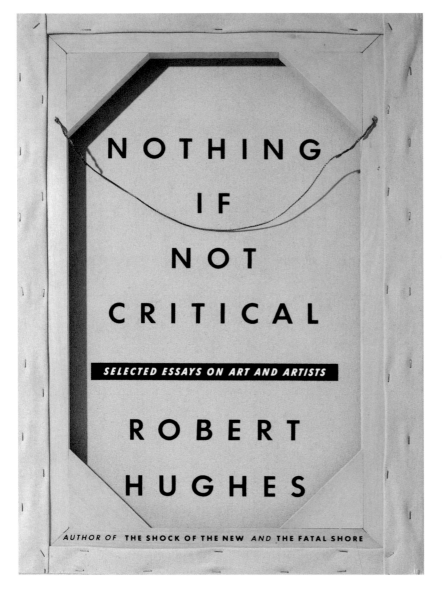

Nothing If Not Critical
Robert Hughes
Photograph – Mark Hill
1992 New York ALFRED A. KNOPF
[Hardback]

Using a painting to illustrate a collection of essays on art and artists would have been too literal – and it would have made the book seem like a monograph on a particular artist. In contrast, the back of a canvas prompts the curiosity of the reader. Author Robert Hughes loved the cover which he described as "a visual epigram, not a piece of hype".[5]

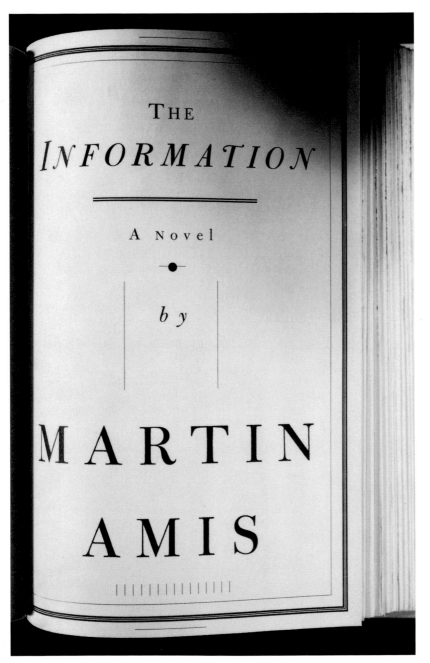

The Information 45
Martin Amis
Photograph – Chip Kidd
1995 New York HARMONY BOOKS
[Hardback]

A bitter satire for our age, this moralistic
tale tells of how information can be
manipulated in the world of contemporary
media and literature. Reminiscent of
an 18th-century pamphlet, the cover
intimates that the author is some kind
of Enlightenment philosopher.

46   *Genet: A Biography*
Edmund White
Photograph of Genet – Brassai
Photograph of picture in frame –
Geoff Spear
1993 New York ALFRED A. KNOPF
[Hardback]

While in a bookstore in East Hampton,
Kidd found this signed photograph
of Genet by Brassai. The selling price
of $3,000 was too much, so Kidd persuaded
the owner to rent him the piece. While
being shipped to his office the glass broke
and Kidd couldn't resist; he photographed
it for the cover just as it was, because, he
says, "The composition was so great, and
Genet was such a rabble rouser."

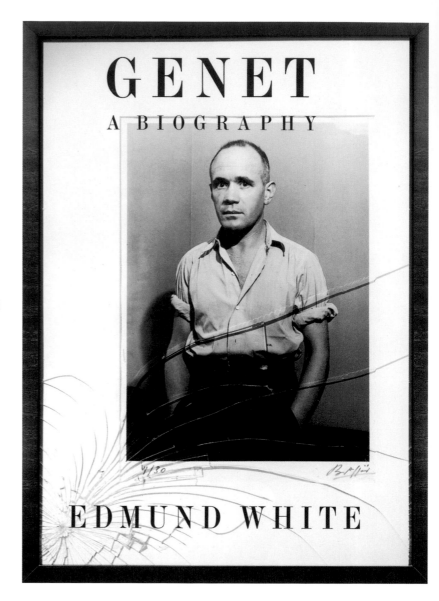

The Marquis de Sade: A Life
Neil Schaeffer
1999 New York ALFRED A. KNOPF
[Hardback]

All the components of the literary legend
are here: the complex, stylized density
of the period, the red slash of daring
transgression and the background of
pervasive and menacing black. Kidd took
a very intuitive approach to the project:
"I tried to imagine what Sade himself
would have done to the cover," he says.

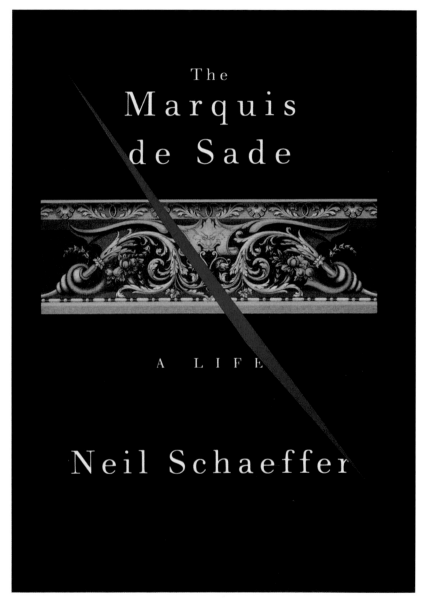

White Jazz
James Ellroy
Photograph – Robert Morrow
1992 New York ALFRED A. KNOPF
[Hardback]

"Chip Kidd frames the front cover in
pristine white – a color at once stark,
innocent and inviting. Centered in that
white expanse: an LAPD patrol car door
shot full of holes. The potential book
buyer/reader has been presented with
a statement and a challenge – forceful,
simple, elegant: Read This Book!"
– *James Ellroy*

The Cold Six Thousand
James Ellroy
Main photograph – Mell Kilpatrick
2001 New York ALFRED A. KNOPF
[Hardback]

48

The blurred colour photograph of a neon
Las Vegas landscape sets the location for
a tale of violence and corruption amid the
desert casinos. The bloodied crime scene
offers a macabre invitation to enter a world
peopled with amoral characters who both
repel and fascinate.

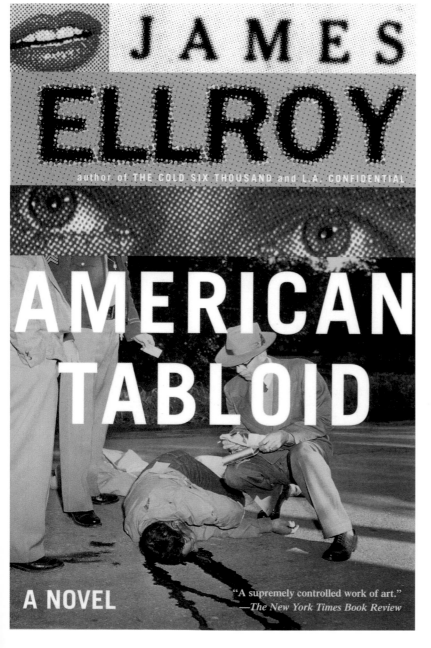

American Tabloid
James Ellroy
Main photograph – Mell Kilpatrick
2001 New York ALFRED A. KNOPF
[Paperback]

49

The saturated and grainy colour images of eyes and lips highlight our voyeuristic attraction to scenes of bloodshed and mayhem. The vintage shot of a crime scene makes reference to the American underworld in the years before and after the Bay of Pigs.

Get Shorty
Elmore Leonard
Photograph – Judah Harris
1998 New York DELACORTE PRESS
[Paperback]

Out of a close working relationship
between Leonard and Kidd came this
typographic signature, almost a brand that
Kidd created and that Leonard has carried
with him from publisher to publisher.

Each of these three titles features one
of Kidd's favourite design solutions, the
graphic collage. Just as readers try to
solve the riddle of the murder mystery,
they are invited to decipher the meaning
of the cover images: Shorty as that
diminutive gentleman, Mr. Majestyk as
a felon in a not-so-majestic prison cell
and the cat chaser as bulldog.

Mr. Majestyk
Elmore Leonard
Photograph – Bastienne Schmidt
2000 New York BANTAM DELL
[Paperback]

Cat Chaser
Elmore Leonard
Photograph – Judah Harris
1998 New York QUILL
[Paperback]

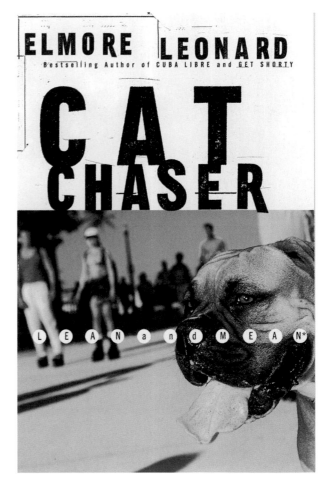

American Rhapsody
Joe Eszterhas
Photograph – Plastock
2000 New York ALFRED A. KNOPF
[Hardback]

To illustrate this virulent attack on the
Clintons, the editor-in-chief of Knopf said:
"Why don't we do a jacket that will give
everybody a big kiss?" The barely open
mouth captures the gossipy, bitchy style
of the book, a tell-all Hollywood meets the
White House rant.

Jurassic Park
Michael Crichton
Illustration – Chip Kidd
1990 New York ALFRED A. KNOPF
[Hardback]

The silhouetted dinosaur skeleton
that eventually became the logo for the
merchandising on the blockbuster film
was Kidd's hand-traced elaboration of
an image that he created for the original
hardcover. Probably one of the most seen
images of the 1990s.

52

Disclosure
Michael Crichton
1994 New York ALFRED A. KNOPF
[Hardback; shown with spine]

The jacket is printed on two layers to
reflect the main theme of the novel
which is concealment. A semi-transparent
stripe of white offsets the red jacket and
"discloses" the book's title on the binding
underneath. The plainness of the aesthetic
cuts through the bookstore clutter of other
more embellished jackets.

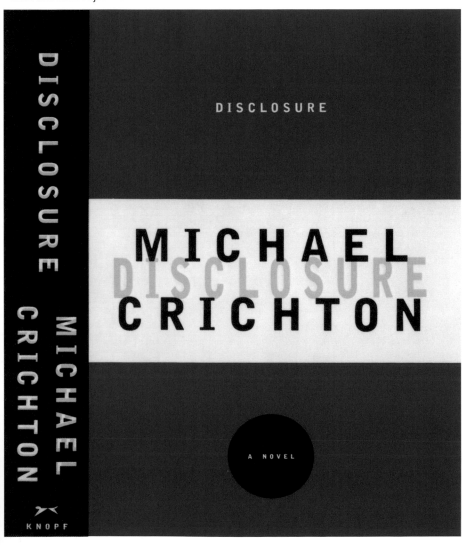

54   *The Abomination*
Paul Golding
Photograph – Lars Klove
2000 New York ALFRED A. KNOPF
[Hardback]

The black and white photograph on the
cover mirrors the unrelenting alienation
of the main character, a child whose
sexual identity makes him an outsider.
An innocent symbol of childhood stood on
its head, this image was on a postcard sent
to Kidd when he was in the middle of
reading the manuscript.

the abomination

a novel

Paul Golding

All You Who Sleep Tonight
Vikram Seth
Photograph – Anton Stokowski
1990 New York ALFRED A. KNOPF
[Hardback]

Seth's subject is everyday life seen
through the prism of his startling poetry.
The cheeky image of cutlery bundled up
for a good night's sleep suggests that
mundane scenarios sometimes have
profound implications. "Thanks for the
cutlery," commented the author when
seeing his cover.

Grey is the Color of Hope
Irina Ratushinskaya
Photograph – Mark Ellidge
1988 New York ALFRED A. KNOPF
[Hardback]

This story tells of how a young female
activist in the Soviet Union tried to retain
her humanity in the face of seven years
of hard labour and five years of internal
exile. "The author wrote this book from
notes on scraps of paper she had written
while in jail," explains Kidd. "The cover
is meant to be very collagey – as if put
together by hand."

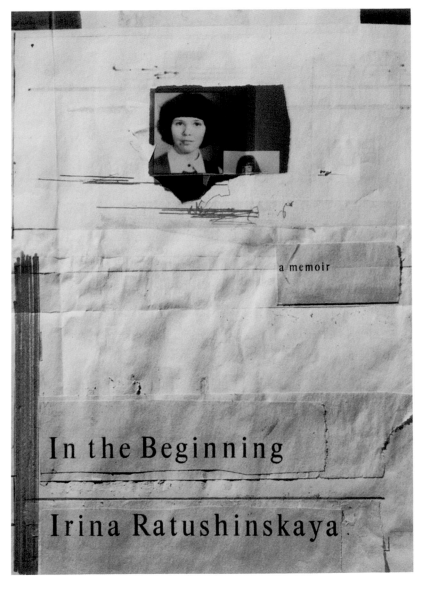

In the Beginning
Irina Ratushinskaya
Photograph – Geoff Spear
1991 New York ALFRED A. KNOPF
[Hardback]

Patched together like a memoir, this cover is a fragile document that suggests the author's state of mind after being released from prison.

57

58 *The English Patient*
Michael Ondaatje
Photograph – Cecil Beaton
1992 New York ALFRED A. KNOPF
[Hardback]

This novel tells of love and alienation, as
characters are each taken out of their own
environment and harshly thrust together
by war. The haunting photograph by Cecil
Beaton is given deep poignancy by an odd
"letterbox" showing a detail from an
Italian Renaissance painting, an oasis in
the midst of an emotional desert, perhaps?

The Little Friend
Donna Tartt
Photograph – Geoff Spear
2002 New York ALFRED A. KNOPF
[Hardback]

In this novel, a precocious 12-year-old girl
tries to solve the mystery surrounding the
death of her younger brother found hanged
in the backyard. The shadows on the doll's
face tell of the potential menace at the
margins of childhood.

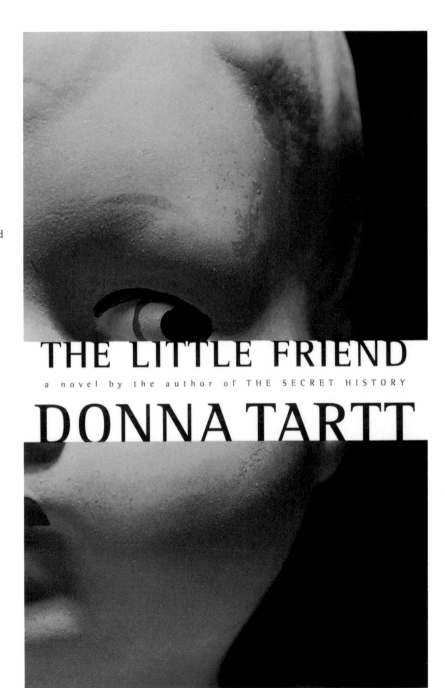

All the
Pretty Horses

Cormac McCarthy

All the Pretty Horses
Cormac McCarthy
Photograph – David Katzenstein
1992 New York ALFRED A. KNOPF
[Hardback]

For the jacket of the first book of what came to be known as *The Border Trilogy*, Kidd wanted a black and white image, reserving sepia and colour for the upcoming titles. "This cover violates one of my cardinal rules which is never to be literal," he adds. "Usually, I would never show a horse if the word horse is in the title. And yet, somehow, it was so right." Indeed, the close-up of the horse's mane echoes McCarthy's ability to create a vividly felt world by bringing to life textures and physical details.

The Crossing

Cormac McCarthy

The Crossing
Cormac McCarthy
Photograph – Melanie Acevedo
1994 New York ALFRED A. KNOPF
[Hardback]

The hard-edged realism of the sepia-toned photograph combined with the stark simplicity of the cover layout prepare the reader for a harsh yet poetic portrait of young man alone as he confronts a barren and hostile landscape.

Cities of the Plain
Cormac McCarthy
Photograph – Larry Schwarn
1998 New York ALFRED A. KNOPF
[Hardback]

A searing colour image of intense beauty sets the scene for this dark tale played out against the vast landscape of the American West. Instead of revealing the double-entendre of the title (an evocation of *Sodom and Gomorrah*) Kidd chose a photograph that reflects the haunting quality of the narrative.

Cities of the Plain

Cormac McCarthy

My Hard Bargain
Walter Kirn
Photographs – Chip Kidd
1990 New York ALFRED A. KNOPF
[Hardback]

"In the first story of this collection,"
explains Kidd, "a group of adolescent
boys in a Mormon school is asked by their
basketball coach to keep track of how
many times they masturbate by making
an ultraviolet star each time on a large
piece of black paper. At the end of the
season, the coach assembles the team,
posts all the papers and, in the darkened
locker room, turns on a big black light.
The story is called 'Planetarium.'"[6]

62

Naked
David Sedaris
Photographs – Peter Zeray/Photonica
1997 New York LITTLE, BROWN & CO
[Hardback]

Sedaris confided in Chip that his favourite
aspect of the design is that when asked
for autographs, he takes off the jacket
and draws a penis on the X-ray.

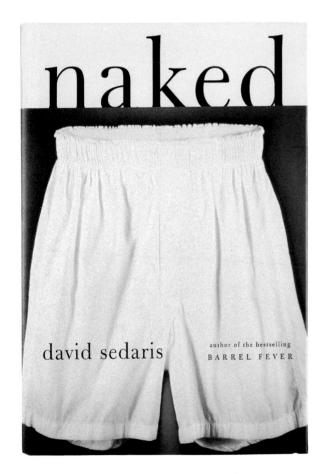

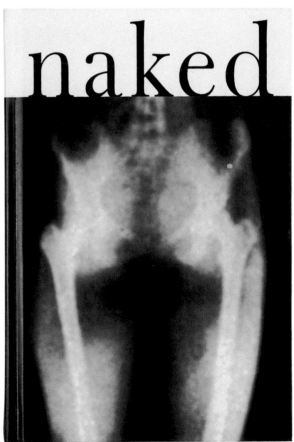

THE NEW TESTAMENT

translated by

RICHMOND LATTIMORE

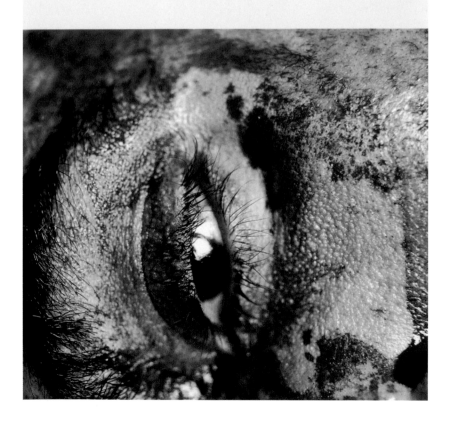

The New Testament
Richmond Lattimore (trans.)
Photograph – Andres Serrano
1996 New York FARRAR, STRAUS
& GIROUX
[Hardback]

"If I am only remembered for one jacket I would pick this one. I really have to hand it to the publisher for having the balls to go with it, and thus getting screwed by the major chains who refused to carry it. I'd also like to thank the photographer for allowing me to use this image in this context."[7]

"People Never Notice Anything"
1992 AIGA BOOK SHOW
Poster

Clowns and religious icons, all grist for
Kidd's mill. He pulls out all the stops to
make sure we *do* notice this poster.

65

66 *The Spectacle of the Body*
Noy Holland
Illustration – James Fish
1995 New York ALFRED A. KNOPF
[Hardback]

The naïve style of illustration suits
the tone of these gothic stories of the
American South, in which characters
slowly reveal their bizarre and alarming
physical obsessions. Though unusual for
Kidd, the illustration on the jacket shows
his confidence with the medium.

My Name is Red
Orhan Pamuk
2001 New York ALFRED A. KNOPF
[Hardback]

This story of murder and intrigue is set
in 16th-century Turkey. The miniatures
on the cover are as richly detailed as the
dense narrative of the novel. This visual
tapestry, in which pictorial snippets are
"woven" together with layers disappearing
under other layers, is not unlike the
complex story that only gradually unfolds.

The Wind-Up Bird Chronicle
Haruki Murakami
Photograph – Geoff Spear
Varnish overlay – Chris Ware
1997 New York ALFRED A. KNOPF
[Hardback]

"Chip and I were in Los Angeles shooting
for the *Batman Animated* book," remembers
photographer Geoff Spear, "when he found
this wind-up bird in a little store on
Melrose called 'The Last Wind-up'. Chip
just said, 'I could use one of these for a
book jacket.' He bought it and we shot it
with a special macro lens."

68

(CONTINUED FROM FRONT FLAP)

"This overwhelming tidal wave of story [is] absolutely
mesmerizing, befuddling, unaccountably
brilliant…[Murakami's] canvas is as broad as
twentieth-century Japan, his brush strokes imbued
with the lines and colors of American pop
culture."   —*Booklist*

"A major work bringing signature themes of
alienation, dislocation, and nameless fears through the
saga of a gentle man forced to trade the familiar for the
utterly unknown…This is a fully mature, engrossing
tale of individual and national destinies entwined. It will
be hard to surpass."
                                    —*Kirkus Reviews*

Haruki Murakami was born in Kyoto in 1949 and now lives near
Tokyo. The most recent of his many honors is the Yomiuri Literary Prize, whose previous recipients include Yukio Mishima, Ken-
zaburō Ōe, and Kōbō Abe. He is the author of the novels *Dance
Dance Dance*, *Hard-Boiled Wonderland and the End of the World*, and *A
Wild Sheep Chase*, and of *The Elephant Vanishes*, a collection of stories. His work has been translated into fourteen languages.

TRANSLATED FROM THE JAPANESE BY JAY RUBIN

Haruki Murakami's *Dance Dance Dance*, *The Elephant Vanishes*, and
Hard-Boiled Wonderland and the End of the World are available in
Vintage paperback.

Jacket photograph by Geoff Spear
Wind-up bird mechanical diagram by Chris Ware for Acme Novelty Productions
Jacket design by Chip Kidd

Alfred A. Knopf, Publisher, New York
http://www.randomhouse.com/

PRINTED IN U.S.A. © 1997 ALFRED A. KNOPF INC.

ISBN 0-679-44669-9 FICTION
52595
9 780679 446699

THE WIND-UP BIRD CHRONICLE

HARUKI MURAKAMI

FPT   U.S.A. $25.95
Canada $36.00

With three novels and one short-story collection now translated into English, Haruki Murakami has emerged as the most significant Japanese novelist in decades. And with this hugely ambitious new book—a true magnum opus, equal in scope and execution to Yukio Mishima's posthumous tetralogy, *The Sea of Fertility*—he will take his place in the international pantheon of contemporary literature.

The Wind-Up Bird Chronicle is many things: the story of a marriage that mysteriously collapses; a jeremiad against the superficiality of contemporary politics; an investigation of painfully suppressed memories of war; a bildungsroman about a compassionate young man's search for his own identity as well as that of his nation. All of Murakami's storytelling genius—combining elements of detective fiction, deadpan humor, and metaphysical truth, and swiftly transforming commonplace realism into surreal revelation—is on full, seamless display. And in turning his literary imagination loose on a broad social and political canvas, he bares nothing less than the soul of a country steeped in the violence of the twentieth century.

Deceptively simple, wise, poignant, funny, and horrifying, *The Wind-Up Bird Chronicle* is a mesmerizing saga of personal conscience and the power of history: a stunning achievement whose impact will be felt worldwide.

ADVANCE REVIEWS

"A surreal, sprawling drama—part detective story, part history lesson, part metaphysical speculation, part satire—that marks Murakami's most ambitious work to date."   —*Publishers Weekly*

"A three-part suspense tale involving war crimes, wells, and the requisite mysterious women—a 640-page book that literally weighs in with *Infinite Jest*, *Mason & Dixon*, and Don DeLillo's *Underworld*."   —*New York*

(CONTINUED ON BACK FLAP)

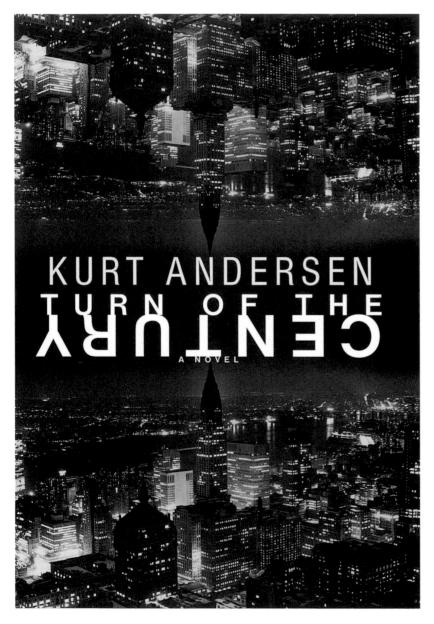

Turn of the Century
Kurt Andersen
Photograph – Corbis/UPI
1999 New York RANDOM HOUSE
[Hardback]

This fictional foray into the media worlds of New York and Los Angeles, with detours via Microsoft, ultimately poses the question of whether life imitates art or art imitates life. The mirror image on the cover goes to the core of this conundrum.

A Handbook for Drowning
David Shields
Designed with Barbara de Wilde
Photograph – David Barry
1991 New York ALFRED A. KNOPF
[Hardback]

"It was such a good title, and good titles like that are very rare," said De Wilde who was first assigned the cover. "Chip came to me and said that he wanted to work on it because he had the best image for it. We sat at my table and worked on the type together. When we were done, we presented the jacket and the approval just sailed through."

Twenty Questions
J.D. McClatchy
Photograph – Max Aguilera-Helwig
1998 New York COLUMBIA UNIVERSITY
PRESS
[Paperback]

Originally taken for the cover of the
catalogue of the Mütter Museum of the
College of Physicians of Philadelphia – a
strange museum of medical abnormalities
– this jacket photograph reaches a new
level of ambiguity thanks to the overlaying
graphic "questions". "Doing design for
one's spouse [J.D. McClatchy] is always a
questionable proposition," says Kidd, "but
I think the result was worth the arguing."[8]

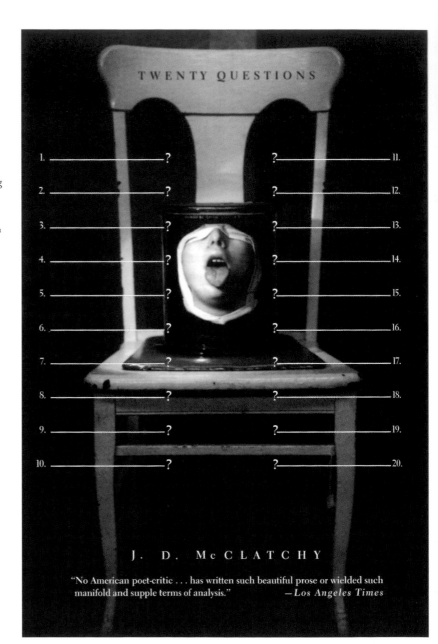

The Elephant Vanishes
Haruki Murakami
Collage – Chip Kidd
1993 New York ALFRED A. KNOPF
[Hardback]

For this collection of short stories that highlight the strangeness of ordinary life, Kidd once again violates his cardinal rule of not being too literal by putting an elephant on the cover. However, the carefully composed mechanical pachyderm is a perfect visual metaphor for the surreal stories within. "The illustration on the front cover is a collage made of art that was swiped from a German beer vat catalog from the 1930s or the 1940s," says Kidd. "And don't ask me why I did this. I don't know. I just did it."

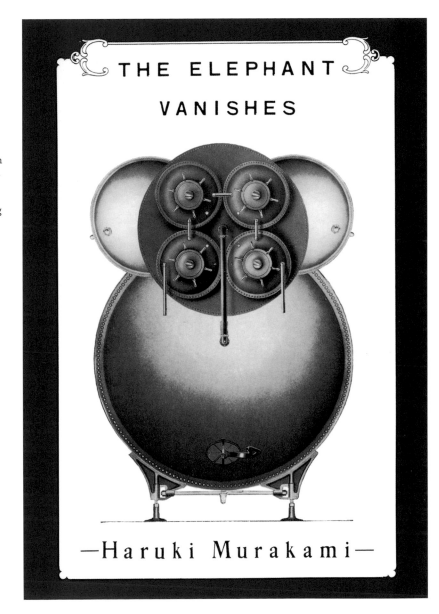

VERTIGO PARK *and other tall tales*

MARK O'DONNELL

Vertigo Park and Other Tall Tales
Mark O'Donnell
Collage – Chip Kidd
1994 New York ALFRED A. KNOPF
[Hardback]

"I've looked at this so many times, the face seems perfectly natural to me," says Kidd. "O'Donnell's humor is by turns outrageous and subtle, dopey and smart. It makes my head spin."[9]

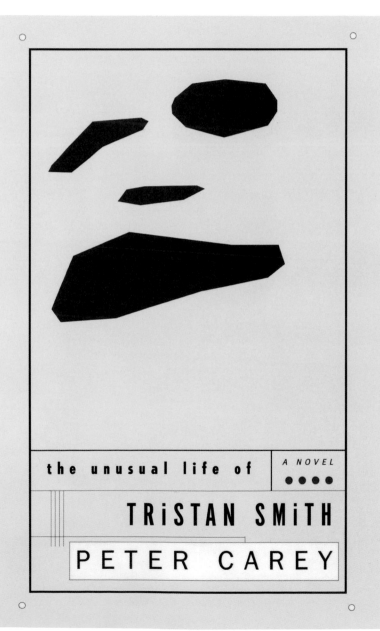

The Unusual Life of Tristan Smith
Peter Carey
1995 New York ALFRED A. KNOPF
[Hardback]

This minimalist jacket is reminiscent
of the more playful work of Paul Rand.
Uncharacteristically, Kidd used a cut
paper technique instead of a conceptual
photograph to depict the hero of the novel,
a malformed but ferociously wilful dwarf
who lives in a nameless future.

75

Awakenings
Oliver Sacks
Photographs – courtesy of Oliver Sacks
1999 New York VINTAGE BOOKS
[Paperback; shown with spine]

To illustrate the central theme of opening
and closing, Kidd contrasts the dull,
downcast eyes in the upper photograph
with the alert gaze of the subject in the
lower photograph. A frieze of brainwave
recordings completes the collage. Sacks
specifies in his contract that Kidd be the
designer of his books – an unusual clause
in any publishing deal.

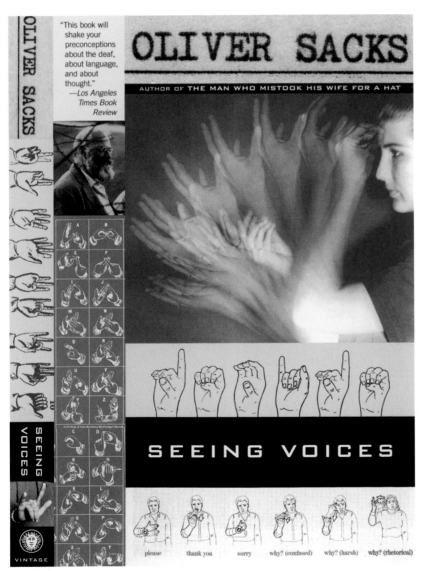

Seeing Voices
Oliver Sacks
Photographs – courtesy of Oliver Sacks
1999 New York VINTAGE BOOKS
[Paperback; shown with spine]

Kidd relates, "Amazingly, for Sacks' previous covers no one had ever thought to look into the extraordinary collection of images from his medical files. I used all the 'indigenous' material, if you will. There was no reason to go outside for illustrations. This stuff is really interesting."

78   *Uncle Tungsten*
Oliver Sacks
Photograph – Geoff Spear
2001   New York   ALFRED A. KNOPF
[Hardback]

This lively memoir of London life recounts
how a boy's curiosity is encouraged by his
scientifically minded Jewish family. The
vibrant colours echo young Sacks' sense of
excitement as he discovers the properties
of metals from his "Uncle Tungsten".

Remaking the World
Henry Petroski
1998 New York ALFRED A. KNOPF
[Hardback]

"For this book on social engineering, I wanted to represent something that looks like a 19th-century fairy tale," explains Kidd. "But when you look closely at the buildings, you recognize them as the ultramodern, tallest skyscrapers in the world, located in Malaysia." The fun and romance of the engineers' quest is conveyed by the playful choice of colours, images and borders.

BILL HAYWARD

THE OLD *Moderns*

KNOPF

DENIS DONOGHUE

ISBN 0-394-58934-3

52750>

9 780394 589343

The Old Moderns
Denis Donoghue
Designed with Barbara de Wilde
1988 New York ALFRED A. KNOPF
[Hardback]

Simplicity of form is the hallmark of the
modern literary style as exemplified by
Donoghue in this collection of essays. Kidd
features on the front cover a selection of
neatly aligned typographical rules, only
to brush them aside on the back cover –
just as modern literature sweeps away all
precedent. Note, on the back of the jacket,
the deliberate relationship between the
typographical rules and the bar code.

82 *Glamorama*
    Bret Easton Ellis
    Photograph – Patrick McMullen
    1999 New York ALFRED A. KNOPF
    [Hardback]

Glamorama features minor celebrities
and their sycophants in a tale of greed,
inanity and violence. The jacket sleeve,
peppered with die-cut gunshots, alludes
to the violence of the nightclub scene.
Through each gunshot, a diminutive cameo
portrait is seen, hinting, perhaps, at the
characters' ultimate insignificance.

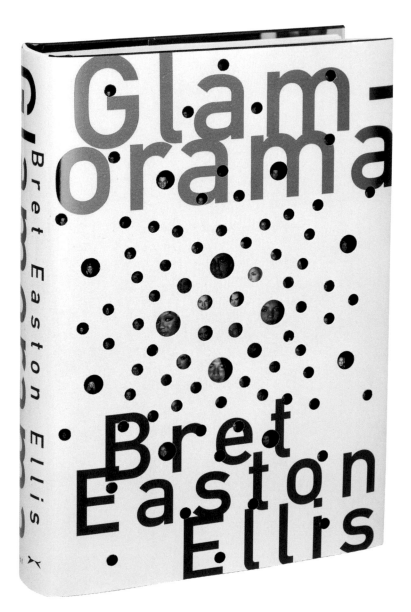

Mixing Messages
Ellen Lupton
1996 New York PRINCETON
ARCHITECTURAL PRESS FOR THE COOPER-
HEWITT NATIONAL DESIGN MUSEUM
[Hardback]

The two main camps in graphic design
are deftly rendered here, the exuberance
of pop commercialism versus the staid
formalism of the academics. Kidd abandons
his trademark horizontal split for the
equally dramatic vertical one.

Pastoralia
George Saunders
2000 London BLOOMSBURY PUBLISHING
[Paperback]

"The author wanted me to do the
hardcover but the publisher was highly
resistant to me working on it, and said
that they didn't have a freelance budget,"
explains Kidd. "Meanwhile they assigned
it to Archie Ferguson who has his office
next door to mine. When I found out,
I called the author who then put pressure
on the publisher to let me try. They
relented – but rejected my design anyway."
In the end, Ferguson's design graced the
American hardcover, but Kidd's jacket
got on the British edition.

Dreaming in Cuban
Cristina Garcia
1992 New York ALFRED A. KNOPF
[Hardback]

This novel details the inner lives of
various members of the del Pino family,
from Cuba to Miami. Carefully choosing
an illustration in a vintage Latin style,
Kidd heightens the tension by obscuring
the lower face of the woman with a bold
red block of colour, preparing the reader
for intimate glimpses into the thoughts
and memories of the predominantly
female characters.

The Agüero Sisters
Cristina Garcia
1997 New York ALFRED A. KNOPF
[Hardback]

Two Cuban sisters are separated; one
embraces the American dream while
the other stays in Cuba and works for
"la revolucion". The pastel-toned
illustration shows a woman looking
upward, presumably representing the
characters' yearning for self-realization.

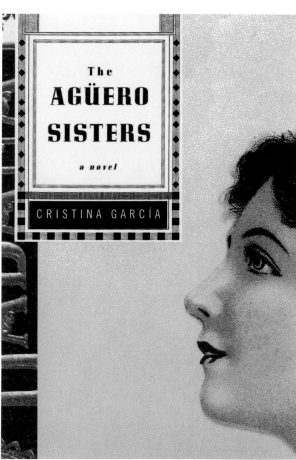

Savage Art
Robert Polito
1995 New York ALFRED A. KNOPF
[Hardback]

This biography of Jim Thompson, author
of many crime novels from the 1940s and
1950s, uses in its cover two key elements of
the noir novel, the gorgeous pin-up blonde
and the weather-beaten detective. In this
two-panel format, two images are featured
at two different scales, a Kidd trademark.

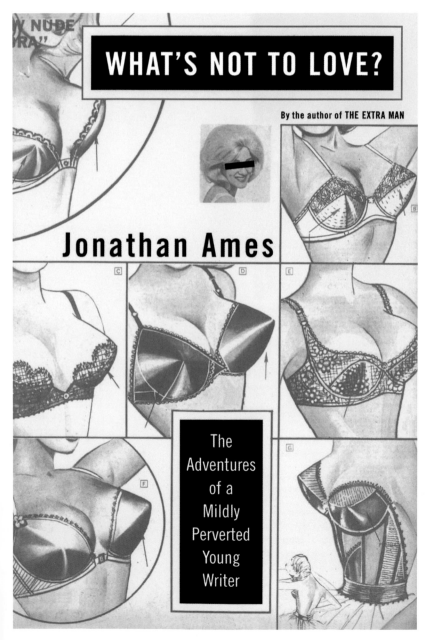

What's Not to Love,
Jonathan Ames
2000 New York CROWN PUBLISHING
[Hardback]

Ames' essays tell of sexual obsession
and crippling shyness. The disjointed
pneumatic female curves from vintage
lingerie illustrations embody the author's
simultaneous feelings of desire and
inability to make real his fantasies.
The "cameo" of the blindfolded model
reinforces this theme.

87

Further Adventures
Jon Stephen Fink
Illustration – Chip Kidd
1993 New York ST. MARTIN'S PRESS
[Hardback]

The subject of this novel, a radio star who
was the voice of a superhero, allows Kidd
to explore his own passion for comic books
and superheroes. The image in a small
medallion inserted into the background
illustration is a device Kidd quite often
uses to disrupt a complacent sense of scale.

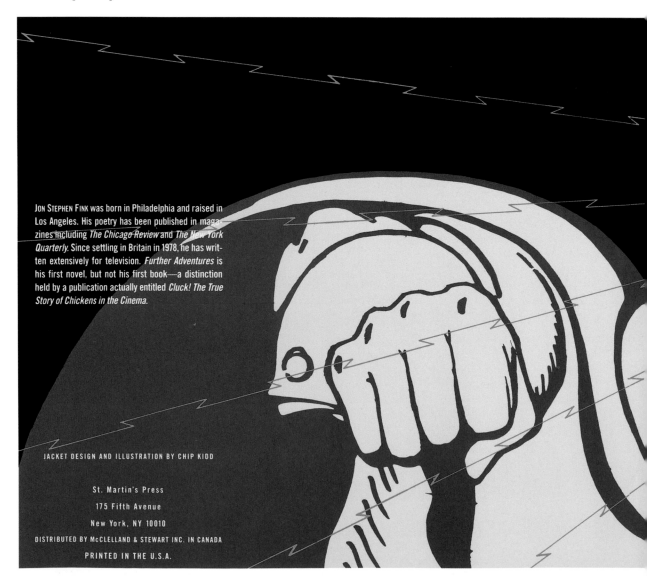

JON STEPHEN FINK was born in Philadelphia and raised in
Los Angeles. His poetry has been published in magazines including *The Chicago Review* and *The New York
Quarterly.* Since settling in Britain in 1978, he has written extensively for television. *Further Adventures* is
his first novel, but not his first book—a distinction
held by a publication actually entitled *Cluck! The True
Story of Chickens in the Cinema.*

JACKET DESIGN AND ILLUSTRATION BY CHIP KIDD

St. Martin's Press
175 Fifth Avenue
New York, NY 10010
DISTRIBUTED BY McCLELLAND & STEWART INC. IN CANADA
PRINTED IN THE U.S.A.

FURTHER ADVENTURES

a novel

JON STEPHEN FINK

ISBN 0-312-09059-5

$14.95

When the Hour of Darkness is upon us—

when all Hope is gone—

he blazes from the shadows to defend the defenseless!

To punish the Criminal!

To purge wrong and keep America strong!

From 1938 to 1946 he was the voice of the Green Ray. Sponsored by P. K. Spiller's High-Energy Buckwheat Breakfast Flakes, he kept Radioland enthralled from sea to shining sea every week—even if behind the echo chamber and all the special effects he was only scrawny little Ray Green, known to his family as Reuven Agranovsky.

Now, four decades later, when a freak accident causes an all-night blackout in the little town of Mason, New Mexico, certain events force the Green Ray out of retirement. But maybe Reuven should have stayed in the shadows; after all sixty-six is no time in life to start thinking you're the only good man in a wicked world, or to get yourself trapped in a gathering nightmare of unspeakable crimes—least of all with the mysterious beauty Amelia Defuentes waiting in the wings to be rescued...

Further Adventures is Jon Stephen Fink's tumbling cavalcade of a first novel, the poignantly funny, hilariously tragic narrative of one man's half-blind but whole-hearted stumble against the forces of greed, perversion and reality. As imaginative and irresistible as John Kennedy Toole's *A Confederacy of Dunces*, it is an absolutely original and entertaining *tour de force*.

The Boomer
Marty Asher
Illustrations from Charles S. Anderson's
CSA Archive
2000 New York ALFRED A. KNOPF
[Hardback]

This boldly experimental work of fiction
chronicles the disaffected life of a typical
baby boomer as he chases after happiness,
finding it briefly at times and then sinking
deeper into his self-involved malaise.
The choice of nostalgic clip art from
Charles Anderson's CSA Archive reflects
how boomers have been influenced, as
well as shaped, by the American consumer
culture. The illustrations float in white
space, suggesting, perhaps, how the
Boomer floats through life without ever
making real connections.

15.

The boomer liked reading. For a while he
thought love, war and death happened only
in books. He especially liked science fiction.

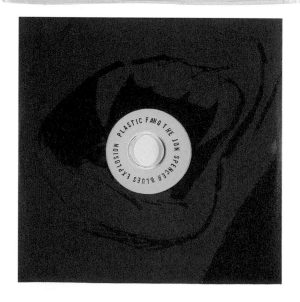

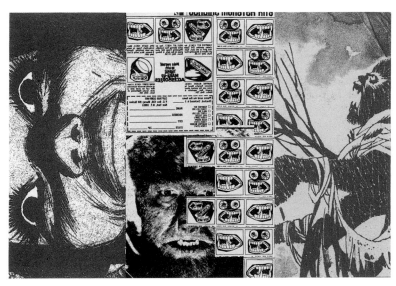

Blues Explosion
OPPOSITE CD cover in bag with
tag and loose CD cover
LEFT Two spreads from CD booklet
2002 MATADOR (US), MUTE (UK)

Kidd really gets his teeth into this one (pun
intended). Here he gives his obsession with
comic book culture free reign. Unfettered
by the narrative form the result is pure
expressive glee.

BATMAN AND ROBIN *Club*

See 14 chapters of "Adventures of Batman and Robin" and have this card punched each week. Then, present the card at the door and see the last chapter ABSOLUTELY FREE!

8	1
9	2
10	3
11	4
12	5
13	6
14	7
FREE 15	

NAME

Chip Kidd

Geoff Spear

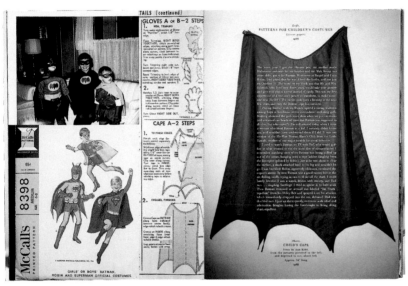

Batman Collected
Chip Kidd
Photographs – Geoff Spear
1996 New York BULFINCH PRESS
[Hardback]
2001 New York WATSON-GUPTILL
[Revised paperback edition; shown here]

Kidd's childhood obsession and lasting
adult passion is Batman. He dates this love
affair to one Halloween when his mother
made him a Batman costume, whose cape
we see pictured on the left. Kidd was not
alone in his obsession. Children across
America not only watched Batman avidly
on television but devoured a whole range
of food products emblazoned with their
hero's likeness.

Kidd and photographer Geoff Spear
document this long-lasting cult in *Batman
Collected*. This cornucopia of Batman
ephemera reads more like a catalogue than
a book. It has no page numbers and is filled
with exuberant collages mixing posters
and packaging with toys and artifacts – all
seen through Spear's dramatic macro lens.

A lavish double gatefold from *Batman
Collected*, showing crude Japanese figures
of the Dynamic Duo. Packaging details,
used as borders, are reminders of the
characters' global reach.

Batman Animated
Paul Dini and Chip Kidd
Drawings – Bruce Timm
1998 New York HARPERENTERTAINMENT/
HARPERCOLLINS
[Hardback]

This book documents the creation of
animated figures from start to finish,
featuring preliminary sketches as well as
the inspiration behind them. The layouts
are glossy patchworks that reflect Kidd's
own appreciation of the complex creative
process behind the television series.

BATMAN=
ANIMATED
PAUL DINI and CHIP KIDD

FORMS STRETCHED TO THEIR LIMITS!

JACK COLE AND PLASTIC MAN

ART SPIEGELMAN and CHIP KIDD

Jack Cole and Plastic Man
Art Spiegelman and Chip Kidd
Illustration – Jack Cole
2001 San Francisco CHRONICLE BOOKS
[Paperback]

The subtitle "Forms Stretched to Their Limits!" could also refer to Kidd's art direction. Panels don't just lie orderly side by side – they float in front, above and behind each other. The cover bears Kidd's trademark horizontal split.

102 *Peanuts: The Art of Charles M. Schulz*
Commentary – Chip Kidd
Introduction – Jean Schulz
Photographs – Geoff Spear
2001 New York PANTHEON BOOKS
[Hardback]

This cover shows the Peanuts gang
peeking over a partial dust jacket as if
over a fence. As Kidd himself comments,
"they're up to their necks in suburban
anxiety". On the slipcover itself, a little
red wagon stands forlorn like the
"Rosebud" sled from *Citizen Kane*; a
symbol of remembered innocence.

The "biographical" double-page spreads
immerse the reader in the minutiae of
Schulz's life – his doodles, his high
school yearbook, his pen ... and the box
it came in.

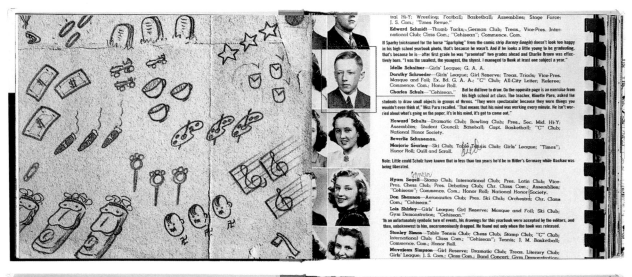

tral Hi-Y; Wrestling; Football; Basketball; Assemblies; Stage Force; J. S. Com.; "Times Revue."

Edward Schmidt—Thumb Tacks; German Club; Treas., Vice-Pres. International Club; Class Com.; "Cehisean"; Commence. Com.

If Sparky (nicknamed for the horse "Sparkplug" from the comic strip *Barney Google*) doesn't look too happy in his high school yearbook photo, that's because he wasn't. And if he looks a little young to be graduating, that's because he is—after first grade he was "promoted" two grades ahead and Charlie Brown was effectively born. "I was the smallest, the youngest, the shyest. I managed to flunk at least one subject a year."

Idelle Schnitzer—Girls' League; G. A. A.

Dorothy Schroeder—Girls' League; Girl Reserve; Treas. Triads; Vice-Pres. Masque and Foil; Ex. Bd. G. A. A.; "C" Club; All-City Letter; Referee; Commence. Com.; Honor Roll.

Charles Schulz—"Cehisean." But he did love to draw. On the opposite page is an exercise from his high school art class. The teacher, Minette Paro, asked the students to draw small objects in groups of threes. "They were spectacular because they were things you wouldn't even think of," Miss Paro recalled. "That means that his mind was working every minute. He isn't worried about what's going on the paper, it's in his mind, it's got to come out."

Howard Schultz—Dramatic Club; Bowling Club; Pres., Sec. Mid. Hi-Y; Assemblies; Student Council; Baseball; Capt. Basketball; "C" Club; National Honor Society.

Beverlie Schuneman.

Marjorie Searing—Ski Club; Table Tennis Club; Girls' League; "Times"; Honor Roll; Quill and Scroll.

Note: Little could Schulz have known that in less than ten years he'd be in Hitler's Germany while Dachau was being liberated.

Hyam Segell—Stamp Club; International Club; Pres. Latin Club; Vice-Pres. Chess Club; Pres. Debating Club; Chr. Class Com.; Assemblies; "Cehisean"; Commence. Com.; Honor Roll; National Honor Society.

Don Shannon—Aeronautics Club; Pres. Ski Club; Orchestra; Chr. Class Com.; "Cehisean."

Lois Shirley—Girls' League; Girl Reserve; Masque and Foil; Ski Club; Gym Demonstration; "Cehisean."

To an unfortunately symbolic turn of events, his drawings for this yearbook were accepted by the editors, and then, unbeknownst to him, unceremoniously dropped. He found out only when the book was released.

Stanley Simon—Table Tennis Club; Chess Club; Stamp Club; "C" Club; International Club; Class Com.; "Cehisean"; Tennis; I. M. Basketball; Commence. Com.; Honor Roll.

Mavajem Simpson—Girl Reserve; Dramatic Club; Treas. Literary Club; Girls' League; J. S. Com.; Class Com.; Band Concert; Gym Demonstration.

He didn't pencil everything in first, as most cartoonists do. "I pencil as little as possible," Schulz said in 1997. "Just enough to get the heights and the space right. But I draw the faces with the pen when I'm doing it. Because you want that spontaneity, you don't want to be just following the pencil line."

He used a 914 Radio, and relied on these pen nibs so much that when the company announced it was going out of business, he bought the entire remaining stock. The hundreds of boxes saw him through the rest of his career.

The homey quality of Kidd's art
direction in these spreads from *Peanuts*
is reminiscent of a family photo album.
Changes of scale give the pages their
texture. The comic strips are photographed
from the original pulp pages, showing
wear and tear and discolouration. Because
Schulz didn't have anything that could be
called an archive in his studio, assembling
this book was like a scavenger hunt for
Kidd and Spear.

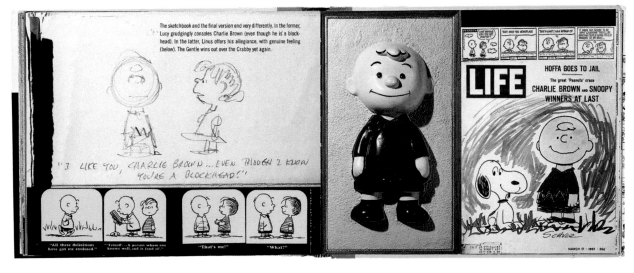

The sketchbook and the final version end very differently. In the former, Lucy grudgingly consoles Charlie Brown (even though he is a blockhead). In the latter, Linus offers his allegiance, with genuine feeling (below). The Gentle wins out over the Crabby yet again.

"I LIKE YOU, CHARLIE BROWN...EVEN THOUGH I KNOW YOU'RE A BLOCKHEAD!"

"All these definitions have got me confused." "'Friend'...A person whom one knows well, and is fond of." "That's me!!" "What?"

HOFFA GOES TO JAIL
The great 'Peanuts' craze
CHARLIE BROWN AND SNOOPY
WINNERS AT LAST

MARCH 17, 1967 · 35¢

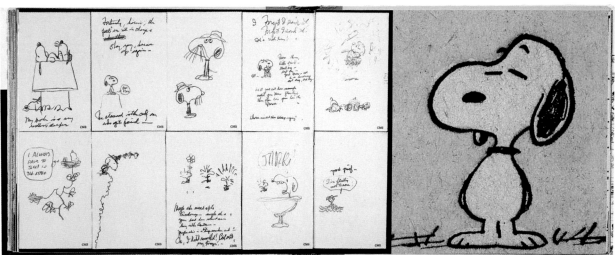

106 *The Cheese Monkeys: A Novel in Two Semesters*
Chip Kidd
Photographs – Geoff Spear
Illustrations – Chris Ware
2001 New York SCRIBNER
[Hardback]

For his own literary debut, a novel set
at the graphic design department of an
American university in the late 1950s,
Kidd used all the gimmicks he always
wanted to use on other people's books.
The typographic cover slips off to show
a second design using pictograms to spell
out the title. And because graphic design
is a key part of the plot, the design of
the book itself becomes a key part of
the narrative. Kidd wrote the text in
QuarkXPress, presumably to visualize how
each page would look as he went along.

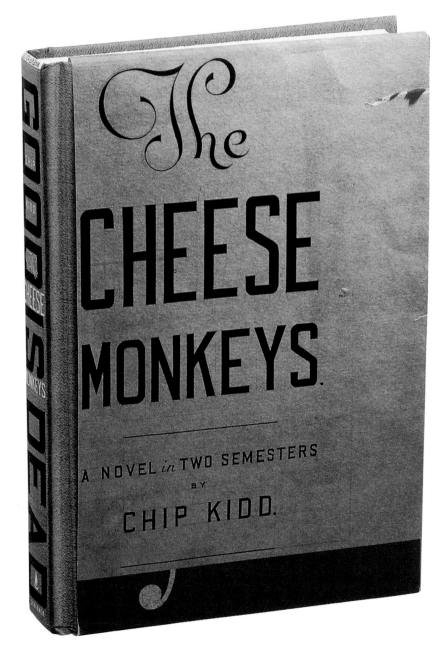

"The narrative gallops along at a breathtaking pace, in part because it's driven by amusingly offbeat people and events, but also because of the book design," writes Julie Lasky. "Kidd has exercised all his skill to fashion a 275-page novel out of what seems like 75 pages of story." [10]

A production challenge, the acknowledgements for *The Cheese Monkeys* teeter along the rim of the cover.

GOOD **CHEESE** IS DEAD.

CHIP KIDD · THE · MONKEYS · SCRIBNER

WHATEVER YOU DO

THE BUGLIUSCO FOUNDATION. MOM AND DAD. MATT. MARY AND THE KIDS. BOMBAY GIN. CHRIS WARE. DAVID RAKOFF. KLEENEX TISSUES.

THE BERKSHIRE MALL. NAN GRAHAM. LYNN GOLDBERG. ALFRED A. KNOPF. JERGINS LOTION. HAND-JOBS MAGAZINE. THE BRIO PIZZA GUY. ANYONE WHO

Notes

The Art of the Jester

1. Tom Wolfe, *The Bonfire of the Vanities*, New York: Farrar, Straus & Giroux, 1987. Jacket designed by Fred Marcellino.

2. See Véronique Vienne, "The Company It Keeps, AIGA 1999 Design Leadership Award to Alfred A. Knopf Inc.", *AIGA Annual No. 19*, p. 47.

3. Derek de Koff, "Captain Kidd", *New York Magazine*, 17 September 2001, p. 42; Calvin Reid, "Designer-Man Wields Pen!", *Publishers Weekly*, 29 September 2001; "The Cheese Monkeys", book review by Julie Lasky, *Print*, no. LVI: 1, March/April 2002, p. 40; Ken Coupland, "Chip Kidd: Between Covers", *Graphis*, no. 338, p. 62.

4. Claire McHugh, "What You See, You Get", *New York Times*, 4 October 1992, v7; John Seabrook, "Bing! It's Fabien", *The New Yorker*, 5 July 1993, p. 74.

5. Derek de Koff, "Captain Kidd", *New York Magazine*, 17 September 2001, p. 42; James Norton, "Going Cover to Cover with Chip Kidd", Flakmag.com, 13 September 2001, www.flakmag.com/features/kidd.html.

6. First published in *I.D.* magazine in the January/February 1993 issue.

7. Alan Powers, *Front Cover: Great Book Jackets and Cover Design*, London: Mitchell Beazley, 2001, p. 110.

8. Brenda Dervin, Ohio State University, "An Overview of Sense-Making Research: Concepts, Methods and Results to Date", paper presented in 1983 to the International Communication Association, Dallas, Texas.

9. Carol Devine Carson eventually emailed me a short list of what she considers Kidd's best covers. *The Abomination* was number three, after *Geek Love* by Katherine Dunn and *The Secret History* by Donna Tartt, which was a collaboration between Kidd and Barbara de Wilde.

10. Quoted from an interview by Cary L. Roberts, "Judging the Author by his Cover", *The Austin Chronicle*, 8 September 2000, p. 54.

11. New York: Harper-Perennial, 1993. Written as a comic book, Scott McCloud's *Understanding Comics* is regarded as a textbook for both art students and comic-strip fans.

12. Ibid, pp. 98–9.

13. "I am well connected in the publishing world and I know how to grease a few palms," admitted Chip Kidd in an interview with Steven Heller published in *Education of a Design Entrepreneur*, New York: Allworth Press, 2002, p. 163.

14. "Chip Kidd: Cover Boy", www.motherjones.com/mother_jones/MJ99/media jones.html.

15. Illustrations from *Batman Collected*, New York: Watson-Guptill, 2001.

16. Chris Ware, *Jimmy Corrigan, or, The Smartest Kid on Earth*, New York: Pantheon, 2002.

17. Quoted from Philip B. Meggs, *A History of Graphic Design*, New York: Van Nostrand Reinhold, 2nd ed., 1992, p. 423.

18. Arthur Koestler is best known for his 1940 novel *Darkness at Noon*. He wrote *The Act of Creation* (London: Hutchinson) in 1964.

19. *Batman: The Complete History*, San Francisco: Chronicle Books, 1999, p. 41.

20. "About the Author, Poets on Poetry", www.randomhouse.com/knopf/authors/mcclatchy.

21. Chip Kidd, *The Cheese Monkeys*, New York: Scribner, 2001, p. 99.

Selected Work

1. Quoted from *Fiction/Non Fiction*, a limited-edition monograph of Chip Kidd's and Barbara de Wilde's work published in 1993 by Glenn Horowitz, East Hampton, New York.

2. Quoted from Ken Coupland, "Chip Kidd: Between Covers", *Graphis*, no. 338, March/April, p. 75.

3. Quoted from Chip Kidd, "Run with the Dwarves and Win: Adventures in the Book Trade", *Print*, May/June 1995, p. 27.

4. Ibid, p. 26.

5. Quoted from *Fiction/Non Fiction*, n.p.

6. Ibid.

7. Quoted from Ken Coupland, "Chip Kidd: Between Covers", p. 75.

8. Quoted from ibid.

9. *Fiction/Non Fiction*, n.p.

10. Julie Lasky, "Word Play: *The Cheese Monkeys: A Novel in Two Semesters*", *Print*, no. LVI: 1, March/April 2002, p. 161.

Selected Bibliography

Books by Chip Kidd

FICTION
The Cheese Monkeys.
New York: Scribner,
2001 (hardcover),
HarperPerennial, 2002
(paperback).

NON-FICTION
*Mythology: The DC Comics
Art of Alex Ross*, New York:
Pantheon, 2003.

Jack Cole and Plastic Man, New
York: Chronicle Books, 2001.
[With Art Spiegelman.]

*Peanuts: The Art of Charles M.
Schulz*, New York: Pantheon,
2001. [Editor and designer.]

Batman Animated, New York:
HarperCollins, 1998. [With
Paul Dini.]

Batman Collected, New York:
Bulfinch Press, 1996
(hardcover), Watson-Guptill,
2001 (paperback).

Articles by Chip Kidd

"We're Off to See the
Wizened", *Hartford Courant*,
Sunday magazine, 19 January
2003, p. 6.

"Superhero Sets Record
Straight", *New York Times*,
op ed, 28 December 2002,
p. A35.

"A Tale of Three Cities", *New
York Times*, 19 May 2002, p. 3.

"September 10: Day of Famy",
New York Observer, 17 December
2001, p. 16.

"I Really Want", *Art & Auction*,
November 2001, p. 111.

"The Bat-Man" (comic-book
story, with art by Tony
Millionaire), *Bizarro Comics*,
2001, no. 1, pp. 55–61.

"Olive or Twist", *New York
Times Magazine*,
5 November 2000, p. 86.

"Trompe Le Garamond", *I.D.*,
May 2000, p. 44.

"Paul Rand", *I.D.*, November
1999, p. 110.

"Confessions of a Window
Dresser" (book review), *I.D.*,
May 1999, p. 96.

"Lanny Sommese: An
Educator Who Is Also
a Successful Practitioner",
Novum, 5 May 1998, pp. 28–35.

"Super", *2wice*, 1998, p. 25.

"Please Don't Hate Him",
Print, May/June 1997,
pp. 42–9.

"Lemonhead", *The New York
Observer*, 10 February 1997,
p. 23.

"Carson City Limits: Design
Lecture Policy in Review", in
Lewis Blackwell, *David Carson:
2nd Sight. Grafik Design after the
End of Print*, London: Laurence
King Publishing, 1997.

"Graphic Details", *American
Vogue*, July 1996, p. 62.

"Fan Mail: Designing Justice
Weekly. Chip Kidd Meets
Kid Vid", *Statements: The
American Center for Design*, fall
1995/winter 1996, pp. 20–1.

"Run with the Dwarves and
Win: Adventures in the Book
Trade", *Print*, May/June 1995,
pp. 21–7.

"You're Going to Need More
Memory", *I.D.*, November
1994, p. 43.

"Very Nice", *Graphis*,
September/October 1993,
pp. 19–20.

"Batman: A Face in the
Dark", www.geocities.com/
SoHo/8652/chipkidd.html.

Articles about Chip Kidd

INTERNET
"About Chip Kidd", www.
dccomics.com/features/plas/
kidd.html.

Baker, John F., "Kidd's Cover:
First Novelist", 7 August
2000, www.publishers
weekly.com/articles/
20000807_88676.asp.

Beach, Karen, "Who Is Chip
Kidd and What Does He Want?",
www.aigaiowa.org/events/
2001/chip_kidd.html.

Birnbaum, Robert,
"Interview: Chip Kidd",
www.identitytheory.com/
people/birnbaum30.html.

"*The Cheese Monkeys* by Chip
Kidd", www.complete-
review.com/reviews/
popus/kiddc.htm.

"*Cheese Monkeys* by Chip Kidd",
28 January 2002, www.the
dailychannel.com/books/
cheesemonkeys.htm.

"Chip Kidd, *Cheese Monkeys,
The* (Scribner)", 2003,
www.theonionavclub.com/
reviews/words/words_c/
cheesemonkeys01.html.

"Discussion: Chip Kidd",
www.globalnetworkofdream
s.com/books/AllAbout/
Chip+Kidd.html.

Green, John, "Kidd, Chip. *The
Cheese Monkeys: A Novel in Two
Semesters*", 1 September 2001,
www.ala.org/booklist/v98/
se1/31kidd.html.

"*Jack Cole and Plastic Man:
Forms Stretched to their
Limits*: by Art Spiegelman
and Chip Kidd", 2001,
www.dccomics.com/
features/plas/.

Kleffel, Rick, "*The Cheese
Monkeys*: Chip Kidd",
2 October 2002, www.trash
otron.com/agony/reviews/
2002/kiddthe_cheese_
monkeys.htm.

Lalumière, Claude, "Bound
Wonder", February 2001,
www.janmag.com/artcult/
wonderwoman.html.

Marc, "Chip Kidd Project
Wins Key Award",
9 August 2002, www.benet.
bertelsmann.com/bnet/
news/spotlight/index/
1,1191,9481_1,00.html.

Norton, James, "Going Cover
to Cover with Chip Kidd",
13 September 2001,
www.flakmag.com/features/
kidd.html.

Ogle, Connie, "The Freshman
Art Major and the Dreaded
Professor", 12 November 2001,
www.miami.com/herald/
content/features/books/
digdocs/092699.htm.

Poynor, Rick, "From Covers
to Content", 2 May 2002,
www.eyemagazine.com/
critique.php?cid=112.

PRINT
AP, "*Batman Collected*: by Chip
Kidd", *Select*, November 1996,
p. 131.

Bark, John, "Slaget Om
Omslaget", *Cap & Design*, 5
September 1996, pp. 46–8.

Barker, Aaron, "Chip Kidd:
An Interview in One Part",
Rough, September 2002,
pp. 1–5.

Blackwell, Lewis, "Batman",
Creative Review, October 1996,
pp. 63–4.

"*The Cheese Monkeys: A Novel
in Two Semesters*", *Publishers
Weekly*, 24 September 2001,
p. 65.

"Chip Kidd", *Fast Company*,
October 1999, p. 129.

"Chip Kidd", *Idea*, no. 281, July
2000, pp. 56–60.

"Chip Kidd", *Idea*, no. 266,
1998, pp. 20–5.

"Chip Kidd", *Idea*, no. 216, September 1989, pp. 43–4.

"Chip Kidd & Barbara de Wilde", *Axis: World Design Journal*, spring 1992, p. 11.

"Chip Kidd and Jon Spencer in Genesis of the Plastic Fang", *Gum*, October 2002, pp. 1–13.

"Chip Kidd: U.S.A.", *Idea Special Edition: Typography-Ex* [PT.02], 2000, pp. 105–9.

Coupland, Ken, "Chip Kidd: Between Covers", *Graphis*, no. 338, March/April 2002, pp. 62–75.

"*The Cheese Monkeys* by Chip Kidd", *Time Out New York*, 11–18 October 2001, p. 65.

Daly, Steve, "*Batman Collected:* Chip Kidd", *Entertainment Weekly*, 1 November 1996, p. 64.

De Koff, Derek, "Captain Kidd", *New York Magazine*, 17 September 2001, pp. 42–5.

Dooley, Michael, "The Grand Inquisitor", *Print*, September/October 1997, p. 28.

Elie, Paul, "Chip Kidd", *Print*, September/October 1992, pp. 105–7.

Feeney, Mark, "Cover Story", *Boston Globe: Living/Arts*, 17 October 2001, p. C1.

Froelich, Janet, "Cover Boy", *New York Times*, 10 November 1996.

Girardi, Peter, "Covered", *Circular: The Magazine of the Typographic Circle*, no. 7, 1997, pp. 6–9.

Goldwasser, Amy, "He's Got You Covered", *Business 2.0*, October 2001, p. 158.

Hall, Peter, "When the Cap Fits", *Creative Review*, February 1993, pp. 27–8.

Helfand, Glen, "Batman Revealed", *Bay Area Reporter: Arts & Entertainment*, 19 December 1996, p. 37.

———, "Fall Art Preview: Chip Kidd", *The Advocate*, 17 September 1996, pp. 55–7.

Hine, Thomas, "Designer Jackets", *New York Times*, 14 October 2001, p. 7.

Hole, Priscilla, "Wilson Alumnus Kidd Illustrates Success for Students", *Reading Eagle: Voices*, 13 August 2002, p. 14.

Holland, Cecelia, "Blowing Up the Museum", *Communication Arts: Advertising Annual*, 1993, pp. 241–3.

"Holy Fixations, Batman", *I.D.*, January/February 1997, p. 30.

"The 100 Smartest New Yorkers", *New York Magazine*, 30 January 1995, pp. 44–5.

"Kidd Stuff", *New York Post*, 8 August 2000, p. 8.

Kipen, David, "Graphic Designer Gives Writing the Old College Try", *San Francisco Chronicle: Datebook*, 24 October 2001, p. E1.

Kuczynski, Alex, "Kidd Crusader", *New York Observer*, 13 November 1996, p. 42.

Lasky, Julie, "Word Play: The Cheese Monkeys: A Novel in Two Semesters", *Print*, no. LVI: 1, March/April 2002, p. 40.

McTavish, Brian, "Here's Looking at You Kidd", *Kansas City Star: Books*, 6 January 2002, p. 16.

Patton, Phil, "Cover Rap", *I.D.*, February 2003, p. 34.

Pryor, Kelli, "Jacket Required", *Entertainment Weekly*, 27 March 1992, p. 68.

Rea, Steven, "Bats about Batman", *Philadelphia Enquirer Magazine: Lifestyle & Entertainment*, 5 December 1996, p. E1.

Reid, Calvin, "Designer-Man Wields Pen!", interview with Chip Kidd, *Publishers Weekly*, 29 September 2001.

Reid, James, "Alumnus Shares Batman Obsession, Collection with University Students", *Daily Collegian: Arts & Entertainment*, 24 January 1997, p. 17.

Roberts, Cary L., "Judge Chip Kidd by his Covers", *Austin Chronicle*, 8 September 2000, p. 54.

Rozzo, Mark, "*The Cheese Monkeys* by Chip Kidd", *Los Angeles Times*, 21 October 2001, p. 10.

Rus, Mayer, "Chip Off the Old Bat", *Out Magazine*, November 1996, p. 62.

Sickler, Ted, "Design Guru Signs Batman Book in New York", *York Daily Record*, 6 December 1996, p. 3D.

Smith, Bill, "The Preservationist: Chip Kidd Speaks", *LA Weekly*, 4–10 January 2002, pp. 29–30.

Terzian, Peter, "Say Cheese", *Newsday: Currents & Books*, 7 October 2001, p. B11.

Treisman, Deborah, "The Bookback Kidd", *Avenue*, January 1994, p. 46.

Yanagihara, Hanya, "Behind the Book: The Series Editor", *Brill's Content*, September 2000, p. 113.

Books Containing Reference to Chip Kidd

Drate, Spencer, Jütka Salavetz, and Mark Smith, *Cool Type*, Cincinnati: North Light Books, 1997.

Fiction/Non Fiction, East Hampton, New York: Glenn Horowitz, 1993.

Heller, Steven, *The Education of a Design Entrepreneur*, New York: Allworth Press, 2002.

———, and Mirko Illic, *Genius Moves: 100 Icons of Graphic Design*, Cincinnati: North Light Books, 2001.

———, and Gail Anderson, *American Typeplay*, New York: PBC International, 1994.

Lupton, Ellen, and J. Abbott Miller, *Design Writing Research*, New York: Princeton Architectural Press, 1996.

Martin, Diana, *Graphic Design: Inspirations and Innovations*, Cincinnati: North Light Books, 1995.

Mixing Messages: Contemporary Graphic Design in America, New York: National Design Museum and Princeton Archictectural Press, 1996. [Exhibition catalogue.]

Mouly, Françoise, *Covering "The New Yorker": Cutting Edge Covers from a Literary Institution*, New York: Abbeville Press, 2000.

Poynor, Rick, *Typography Now Two: Implosion*, London: Booth-Clibborn Editions, 1996, p. 47.

———, *The Graphic Edge*, London: Booth-Clibborn Editions, 1993, p. 191.

U.S. Design 1975–2000, Prestel Verlag/Denver Art Museum, 2001. [Exhibition catalogue.]